D1481373

Industrialization Through the Great Depression

American History Series

Authors: Cindy Barden and Maria Backus

Consultants: Schyrlet Cameron and Suzanne Myers

Editors: Mary Dieterich and Sarah M. Anderson

Proofreader: Margaret Brown

COPYRIGHT © 2011 Mark Twain Media, Inc.

ISBN 978-1-58037-583-2

Printing No. CD-404140

Mark Twain Media, Inc., Publishers
Distributed by Carson-Dellosa Publishing LLC

Visit us at www.carsondellosa.com

Table of Contents

Table of Contents (cont.)

About the American History Series

Industrialization Through the Great Depression is one of the books in Mark Twain Media's new *American History Series.* This book focuses on the events ranging from industrialization, including the development of the steam engine and electricity, to the Roaring '20s. Students will then learn how the Stock Market Crash of 1929 led to the Great Depression, and how the country coped with this economic disaster. This series is designed to provide students in grades 5 through 8 with opportunities to explore the significant events and people that make up American history. Other books in the series include *Exploration, Revolution, and Constitution*; *Westward Expansion and Migration;* and *Slavery, Civil War, and Reconstruction.*

The books in this series are written for classroom teachers, parents, and students. They are designed as stand-alone material for classrooms and home schooling. Also, the books can be used as supplemental material to enhance the history curriculum in the classroom, as independent study, or as a tutorial at home.

The text in each book is presented in an easy-to-read format that does not overwhelm the struggling reader. Vocabulary words are boldfaced. Each book provides challenging activities that enable students to explore history, geography, and social studies topics. The activities promote reading, critical thinking, and writing skills. As students learn about the people who influenced history, they will draw conclusions; write opinions; compare and contrast historical events, people, and places; analyze cause and effect; and improve mapping skills. The research and technology activities will further increase their knowledge and understanding of historical events by using reference sources or the Internet.

The easy-to-follow format of the books facilitate planning for the diverse learning styles and skill levels of middle-school students. National standards addressed in each unit are identified and listed at the beginning of the book, simplifying lesson preparation. Each unit provides the teacher with alternative methods of instruction: reading exercises for concept development, simple hands-on activities to strengthen understanding of concepts, and challenging research activities to provide opportunities for students to expand learning. A bibliography of suggested resources is included to assist the teacher in finding additional resources or to provide a list of recommended reading for students who want to expand their knowledge.

The *American History Series* supports the No Child Left Behind (NCLB) Act. The books promote student knowledge and understanding of history concepts. The content and activities are designed to strengthen the understanding of historical events that have shaped our nation. The units are correlated with the National History Standards for United States History (NHS) and Curriculum Standards for Social Studies (NCSS).

Unit Planning Guide

National Standards Matrix

Each unit of study in the book *Industrialization Through the Great Depression* is designed to strengthen American history literacy skills and is correlated with the National History Standards (NHS) and Curriculum Standards for Social Studies (NCSS).

	Unit 1	Unit 2	Unit 3
National History Standards			
Standard 1: Chronological Thinking	X	X	X
Standard 2: Historical Comprehension	X	X	X
Standard 3: Historical Analysis and Interpretation	X	X	X
Standard 4. Historical Research Capabilities	X	X	X
Curriculum Standards for Social Studies			
Standard 1: Culture	X	X	X
Standard 2: Time, Continuity, and Change	X	X	X
Standard 3: People, Places, and Environments	X	X	X
Standard 4: Individual Development and Identity	X	X	X
Standard 5: Individuals, Groups, and Institutions	X	X	X
Standard 6: Power, Authority, and Governance	X	X	X
Standard 7: Production, Distribution, and Consumption	X	X	X
Standard 8: Science, Technology, and Society	X	X	X
Standard 9: Global Connections	X		X
Standard 10: Civil Ideals and Practices	X	X	X

Suggested Resources

Arnold, James R. and Roberta Weiner. *The Industrial Revolution: The Revolution Comes to America*. Danbury, CT: Grolier, Inc. 2005.

Bagley, Katie. *The Early American Industrial Revolution, 1793–1850*. Mankato, MN: Capstone Press. 2003.

Brezina, Corona. *The Industrial Revolution in America: A Primary Source History of America's Transformation Into an Industrial Society*. New York: The Rosen Publishing Group, Inc. 2005.

Connolly, Sean. *The Industrial Revolution*. Chicago: Heinemann-Raintree Library. 2003.

Cooper, Michael L. *Dust to Eat: Drought and Depression in the 1930s*. New York: Clarion Books. 2004.

Corrigan, Jim. *The 1920s Decade in Photos: The Roaring Twenties*. Berkeley Heights, NJ: Enslow Publishing, Inc. 2010.

Corrigan, Jim. *The 1930s Decade in Photos: Depression and Hope*. Berkeley Heights, NJ: Enslow Publishing, Inc. 2010.

Doak, Robin S. *Black Tuesday: Prelude to the Great Depression*. Mankato, MN: Compass Point Books. 2008.

Feinstein, Stephen. *The 1920s From Prohibition to Charles Lindbergh*. Berkeley Heights, NJ: Enslow Publishing, Inc. 2006.

Freedman, Russell. *Children of the Great Depression*. New York: Clarion Books. 2005.

Halpern, Monica. *Moving North: African Americans and the Great Migration, 1915–1930*. Des Moines, IA: National Geographic Children's Books. 2005.

Hamen, Susan E. *Industrial Revolution*. Vero Beach, FL: Rourke Publishing, LLC. 2010.

Ingram, Scott. *The Stock Market Crash of 1929*. Milwaukee, WI: Gareth Stevens Publishing. 2005.

Levy, Janey. *The Erie Canal: A Primary Source History of the Canal That Changed America*. New York: The Rosen Publishing Group, Inc. 2003.

Levy, Patricia. *From Speakeasies to Stalinism*. Chicago: Raintree. 2006.

O'Neal, Michael J. *America in the 1920s*. New York: Facts on File. 2006

Price, Sean. *Smokestacks and Spinning Jennys*. Chicago: Raintree. 2007.

Rice, Earle. *FDR and the New Deal*. Newark, DE: Mitchell Lane Publishers, Inc. 2009.

Schultz, Stanley. *The Great Depression: A Primary Source History*. Milwaukee, WI: Gareth Stevens Publishing. 2006.

Sioux, Tracee. *Immigration, Migration, and the Industrial Revolution*. New York: Rosen Classroom. 2004.

Swisher, Clarice. *Women of the Roaring Twenties*. San Diego, CA: Lucent Books. 2005.

UXL *Industrial Revolution Reference Library* Series. Farmington Hills, MI: UXL. 2003.

Vander Hook, Sue. *The Dust Bowl*. Edina, MN: ABDO Publishing Company. 2009.

Worth, Richard. *Teetotalers and Saloon Smashers: The Temperance Movement and Prohibition*. Berkeley Heights, NJ: Enslow Publishing, Inc. 2009.

Time Line of Industrialization

1698   Thomas Savery builds a steam engine that can pump water out of flooded mines.

1712   Thomas Newcomen builds his first steam engine.

1764   James Hargreaves develops the spinning jenny.

1764   James Watt invents a separate condenser steam engine.

1782   James Watt builds a steam engine that can produce rotary motion.

1793   Samuel Slater opens the first working U.S. cotton mill.

1793   Eli Whitney invents the cotton gin.

1797   Eli Whitney contracts to make 10,000 muskets for the U.S. Army using interchangeable parts and mass production methods.

1804   Richard Trevithick builds the first steam locomotive that can run on rails.

1807   Robert Fulton's steamboat, the *Clermont*, travels between New York City and Albany.

1817   Work begins on the Erie Canal.

1825   The Erie Canal is completed.

1829   George Stephenson builds the *Rocket,* a steam locomotive that can reach 30 mph.

1831   Michael Faraday invents the dynamo, an early type of electric generator.

1837   Samuel Morse invents the magnetic telegraph.

1844   Samuel Morse sends a message by telegraph from Washington, D.C., to Baltimore.

1850   Isaac Singer produces the first successful sewing machine.

1851   The Great Exhibition in London becomes the model for all World's Fairs to come.

1851   The Bessemer steel-making process is developed.

1857   A New York department store installs the first safety elevator.

1859   The first oil well is drilled.

1862   Louis Pasteur shows how germs cause disease.

1868   Christopher Sholes invents the first practical typewriter.

1868   George Westinghouse invents air brakes for trains.

1869   The first transcontinental railway is completed in the United States.

1876   Alexander Graham Bell invents the telephone.

1877   Thomas Edison invents the phonograph.

1879   Thomas Edison perfects an incandescent light bulb.

1885   Karl Benz builds one of the first gasoline-powered automobiles.

1885   The first skyscraper is built in Chicago.

1888   Heinrich Hertz discovers radio waves.

1888   George Eastman introduces a hand-held box camera for portable use.

1901   Guglielmo Marconi sends radio waves across the Atlantic Ocean.

1903   The Wright Brothers make the first successful airplane.

1908   The first Model T Ford is built.

UNIT ONE: INDUSTRIALIZATION

Name: _____ Date: _____

Industrialization Time Line Activity

Directions: Use information from the time line to answer the questions below. Check the event in each group that came first.

1. _____ Eli Whitney invents the cotton gin.
   _____ The first oil well is drilled.

2. _____ The first skyscraper is built.
   _____ The Erie Canal is completed.

3. _____ Heinrich Hertz discovers radio waves.
   _____ Thomas Newcomen builds his first steam engine.

4. _____ Louis Pasteur shows how germs cause disease.
   _____ James Hargreaves develops the spinning jenny.

5. _____ Samuel Slater opens the first working U.S. cotton mill.
   _____ Samuel Morse invents the magnetic telegraph.

6. _____ The first Model T Ford is built.
   _____ Work began on the Erie Canal.

7. _____ The Wright Brothers make the first successful airplane.
   _____ Isaac Singer produces the first successful sewing machine.

8. _____ A New York department store installs the first safety elevator.
   _____ The first transcontinental railway is completed in the United States.

9. _____ Thomas Edison invents the phonograph.
   _____ Heinrich Hertz discovers radio waves.

10. _____ Alexander Graham Bell invents the telephone.
    _____ The first skyscraper is built in Chicago.

Fill in the Blanks

1. _____ _____ invented air brakes for trains.

2. Michael Faraday invented the _____.

3. Christopher Sholes invented the first practical _____.

4. _____ _____ built his first steam engine in 1712.

5. The _____ steel-making process was developed in 1851.

6. Karl Benz built one of the first gasoline-powered _____.

UNIT ONE: INDUSTRIALIZATION

Name: _____ Date: _____

Industrialization

The word *industrialization* refers to the process of using **power-driven** machinery to manufacture goods. Industrialization has provided tremendous benefits for people, but it has also created great hardships, especially in the past. You will be learning about the many aspects of industrialization in this book.

For hundreds of years, people used muscle power, wind power, and water power to help them in their daily work. Most people depended on the land to grow food or raise sheep and cattle. Then, during the 1700s, people in Britain began to find better ways to farm, to make cloth and metals, and to transport people and goods. In 1782, James Watt, a Scottish engineer, perfected the **steam engine**. Steam engines, which were fueled by coal, provided the first reliable source of power. Manufacturers soon put steam engines to work running all sorts of machinery.

Once steam engines were available, people no longer depended on the land. More people left their small family farms and moved to cities to work in industry. There was so much industrialization going on during the 1700s and the 1800s that this time period is sometimes called the **Industrial Revolution**.

The word *revolution* makes it sound like there was a very sudden change. That's not true. The changeover from human power to machine power had been going on very gradually for 200 years before the Industrial Revolution. All the changes that occurred during the Industrial Revolution were due to the ideas and discoveries of people who had lived long before that time.

The Industrial Revolution started in Britain. Then it spread to the rest of Europe, the United States, and the rest of the world. If you think about it, you will realize that industrialization continues right into our present time.

 *(UNIT ONE: INDUSTRIALIZATION)*

Critical Thinking

The word *revolution* gives the idea of a sudden change. Did the Industrial Revolution start up in a specific year? Give specific details or examples to support your answer.

_____

_____

_____

_____

_____

_____

Name: _____   Date: _____

What Is a Machine?

Critical Thinking

Directions: Answer the questions below. Use your own paper if you need more room.

1. What is a machine? Use your own words to write a definition. _____
   _____

2. List six machines that you have in your home. _____
   _____

3. Which one would you most *not* want to part with? Why not? _____
   _____
   _____

4. How do these machines make your life easier? _____
   _____
   _____

5. How could machines make people's lives more complicated? _____
   _____
   _____

6. Thousands of years ago, people invented simple machines that made lifting and moving heavy loads much easier. The ancient Egyptians used levers and wedges to build the pyramids. In the Middle Ages, people used pulleys to construct the towers on cathedrals. These early machines made work much easier, but they still required manual labor, that is, human muscle power. What machines do you have in your home that require some "muscle power"?
   _____
   _____

7. Before 1700, most people in Europe lived in rural areas and used homemade products. Although there were a few simple factories where people worked together to make luxury items, such as cloth laced with gold thread, there was little industry. What does *industry* mean?
   _____
   _____

8. Besides their own muscle power and animal power, people had two other power sources: water and wind. How can wind be a source of power? How could water be a source of power?
   _____
   _____
   _____

Name: _____   Date: _____

Water Power

Waterwheels were used in Europe for hundreds of years to grind grain, pound rags to make paper, drive hammers for metalworking, power saws, tan leather, treat cloth, and hoist stone and coal from quarries and mines.

During the 1700s, thousands of water-powered mills were also built in America. These mills were used to saw logs into lumber, to clean homespun wool fabric, and to do many other jobs.

There were several types of water-wheels. One type was called the **overshot wheel**. Water from the stream or river was brought to the top of the wheel by a flume or sluice. The water filled the "buckets" that were attached to the wheel. The weight of the water in the buckets pushed the wheel downwards. The buckets emptied out at the bottom and returned to the top empty. The buckets filling and emptying kept the wheel rotating. The center of the wheel was attached to one end of a shaft. The other end of the shaft was attached to gears.

In the picture below, the gears are attached to two grinding stones. Wheat or oats could be dumped into the top of the grinding stones. The motion of the grinding stones would crush the grain into flour. The flour would come out near the bottom of the grinding stones and be put into bags.

Diagram

Directions: Look at the illustration below. Write the words from the box on the correct lines.

stream	shaft	sluice	buckets
gears	flour	wheel	grinding stones

A. _____

B. _____

C. _____

D. _____

E. _____

F. _____

G. _____

H. _____

Name: _____ Date: _____

Inventions

One of the reasons why industrialization occurred was that there were so many new inventions. Competitions with prizes were even set up to encourage inventors.

Cooperative Learning

Directions: Answer each question below. You may work with a partner. Then share your ideas with your classmates.

1. What does it mean to *invent* something? _____
   _____
   _____

2. Why do you think people invent things? _____
   _____
   _____
   _____

3. A well-known saying is "Necessity is the mother of invention." What do you think this saying means? _____
   _____
   _____
   _____

4. Do inventions just "spring out" of people's heads, or are they more likely a result of improvements to other inventions? Give examples to support your ideas.
   _____
   _____
   _____
   _____

5. Circle the qualities that an inventor needs.

   observant   curious   resourceful   clever   intelligent   patient

6. In your opinion, are there other qualities that are more important? What are the two most important qualities for an inventor? _____
   _____
   _____
   _____

Name: _____ Date: _____

Your Invention

Critical Thinking

Directions: Answer the questions below. Use your own paper if you need more room.

1. If you were to invent something, what would it be? _____

_____

2. What would your invention do? _____

_____

_____

3. What would you call your invention? _____

4. How would your invention improve your life or another person's life? _____

_____

_____

Diagram

Directions: Draw a picture of your invention in the picture frame below. Label the parts of your invention.

Name: _____ Date: _____

Standardized Parts

Although it is satisfying to own or make unique things, what would happen if your family's car was slightly different from every other make or model of the same car? How would you replace a faulty steering column or a broken headlight? For things like cars and computers, **uniformity** makes parts **interchangeable**.

Eli Whitney was the nineteenth-century inventor who first put into practice the idea of standardized parts. **Standardized parts** are all made exactly the same. Before his time, everything was made individually. Each item was slightly different from every other item of its kind.

Graphic Organizer

Directions: Complete the vocabulary chart by creating a definition, using the word in a sentence, and drawing an illustration that helps you remember the meaning of the word.

Word	Definition	Illustration
uniformity		
	Sentence	
Word	Definition	Illustration
interchangeable		
	Sentence	

Critical Thinking

How do you think standardized parts influenced American manufacturing? Give specific details or examples to support your answer.

_____

_____

_____

_____

_____

_____

Eli Whitney's Solutions

In 1797, the United States feared it might soon be at war with France, so the government wanted to obtain 40,000 muskets. Fortunately, the war did not happen. This event, however, inspired Eli Whitney to find a way to manufacture guns more efficiently. Before that time, each gun was individually made by a skilled gunsmith. If a part broke, the replacement part had to be custom-made for that gun. Whitney realized that if each gun had interchangeable parts, then it would be easy to replace broken parts.

There was also a shortage of skilled gunsmiths in the country at the time. Whitney designed the kind of machines that could be run by unskilled workers.

Eli Whitney set up a gun factory in 1798. He wanted to produce 10,000 muskets for the U.S. government. Some people didn't think his idea of interchangeable parts would work. Whitney set up a demonstration for President Thomas Jefferson in 1801. He gave Jefferson and some other government officials piles of musket parts. They randomly chose parts from the piles and gave them to Whitney. He was able to put several muskets together very quickly to prove that his idea worked.

Whitney's idea of interchangeable parts had been used in France several decades before his invention. No one had paid much attention to it. Whitney, however, promoted what he called the "American system." He made interchangeable parts important to mass production. Soon, other gun manufacturers in America and England were using his system. Clock makers began to use interchangeable parts as well.

UNIT ONE: INDUSTRIALIZATION

Graphic Organizer
Directions: Complete the chart below. Fill in the solution for each problem.

Problem	Solution
Problem #1: Replacement parts for guns had to be custom-made.	
Problem #2: There was a shortage of skilled gunsmiths in the country at the time.	
Problem #3: People doubted that interchangeable parts would work.	

Name: _____ Date: _____

Learning Textile Terms

Graphic Organizer

Directions: Complete the vocabulary chart by creating a definition, using the word in a sentence, and drawing an illustration that helps you remember the meaning of the word.

Word	Definition	Illustration
waterwheel	Sentence	
Word	Definition	Illustration
textile	Sentence	
Word	Definition	Illustration
loom	Sentence	
Word	Definition	Illustration
weave	Sentence	

Name: _____   Date: _____

How Do You Make Clothes?

Even though textile mills began to change the way people made clothes, American women usually made the clothes for everyone in their families until at least 1810. If you have ever made an article of clothing, you know that it is a lot of work!

Constructed Response

1. Have you ever sewn a shirt or a pair of pants? _____

2. Do you know anyone who sews *all* the clothes for his or her family? Who? _____
   _____

3. The list below shows the steps American women once did to make an item of clothing. The list is not in the right order, however. Number the items in sequential order.

   _____   Sew the pieces by hand into pants, shirts, and skirts.

   _____   Obtain cotton fiber.

   _____   Weave the yarn into cloth.

   _____   Spin the clean cotton fiber into yarn.

   _____   Cut the cloth into pieces.

   _____   Make a pattern

Graphic Organizer

Directions: Complete the chart below. List several advantages and disadvantages of making your own clothes.

Advantages	Disadvantages

Name: _____ Date: _____

Eli Whitney's Cotton Gin

Eli Whitney learned about the problems of **ginning**, or cleaning, cotton while he was visiting an estate in Georgia. The kind of cotton that grew well in the South was called green seed cotton. The seed of this kind of cotton was almost impossible to separate from the cotton fibers. A slave could only clean one pound of green seed cotton a day.

Plantation owners wanted to find a way to **export**, or send, the cleaned cotton to textile mills in England so that they could make a profit. Inventors had already invented gins to separate the cotton fibers from the seed of the plant. However, those machines were not effective because the seed of the green seed cotton plant clung so tightly to the cotton fibers.

In 1793, Eli Whitney invented a cotton gin that cleaned the cotton much more quickly and much better. As a result, growing cotton soon became profitable. Plantation owners wanted *more* slaves so they could grow even more cotton. Both young and old people who were not strong enough to work at other types of jobs started to work ginning cotton. People paid their debts, and land increased in value. Factories in the North started to use the cotton to make cloth. The shipping industry grew as well.

Cause and Effect

Directions: A **cause** is an event that produces a result. An **effect** is the result produced. Write five effects for the cause listed below.

Cause: Eli Whitney invents the cotton gin.

Effect #1 _____

_____

Effect #2 _____

_____

Effect #3 _____

_____

Effect #4 _____

_____

Effect #5 _____

_____

Name: _____   Date: _____

Early American Factories

In 1793, **Samuel Slater** built the first real American **textile** mill in Pawtucket, Rhode Island. In a sense, he began the American Industrial Revolution. Slater put several of the processes that were needed to make textiles into one factory. He used a single waterwheel system to power all the machines.

Almost all of the 30 employees in Samuel Slater's mill were children. He employed children who were seven to 12 years old to work in his mill. The textile machines were easy to operate, so the children did not need any special skills to run them. In those days, children were already working long hours on their family farms, so no one objected to their working in a mill. Soon other factories started, and more than half of the workers in Rhode Island were children.

The children worked alongside adults in terrible conditions. They started working before sunrise and finished after sunset. An overseer supervised them and often used **corporal punishment**.

The mills were always dirty and noisy. In winter, the mills were cold and drafty; in summer, they were hot and humid. Many people developed **respiratory** diseases because of breathing flying lint particles. Although the machines were easy to operate, they were dangerous. If a child was tired or sleepy, he or she could easily lose a finger, an arm, and sometimes, even a scalp!

Samuel Slater

The children lived in housing that Slater built for them. Then he made them buy everything they needed at his company store. Instead of giving them money for their work, he gave them **credits** to use at his store. He tried to control every part their lives. He controlled how long the children worked and how much money they made. He also built churches and schools near his mill. He made sure that the schools taught what he wanted the children to learn.

Back then, only wealthy children had formal schooling. The children who worked in the mills studied basic reading, writing, and arithmetic at Sunday school on their only day off from the mill.

UNIT ONE: INDUSTRIALIZATION

Early American Factories (cont.)

Directions: Complete the following activities.

Matching

_____ 1. corporal punishment

_____ 2. respiratory

_____ 3. textile

_____ 4. Samuel Slater

_____ 5. credits

a. given in place of money

b. having to do with breathing

c. cloth

d. began the American Industrial Revolution

e. infliction of physical pain as a method of changing behavior

Fill in the Blanks

1. _____ _____ built the first real American textile mill.

2. Almost all of the 30 employees in Samuel Slater's mill were _____.

3. The children who worked in the mills studied basic reading, writing, and arithmetic on their only _____ off from the mill.

4. Children started working before _____ and finished after _____.

5. Samuel Slater used a single _____ system to power all the machines.

True or False

Circle "T" for True or "F" for False.

1. T   F   Slater's textile mill was a safe place for children to work.

2. T   F   The textile machines were easy to operate.

3. T   F   Samuel Slater built the first real American textile mill in Pawtucket, New York.

4. T   F   Many people developed respiratory diseases working in the mill because of breathing in flying lint particles.

5. T   F   No one objected to children working in Slater's mill.

Constructed Response

The mill was a dangerous place for children to work. Why didn't anyone object to children working there? Give specific details or examples to support your answer.

_____

_____

_____

_____

_____

Name: _____ Date: _____

Working at Samuel Slater's Textile Mill

Journaling

Directions: Imagine that you lived in 1796 and had to work in Samuel Slater's textile mill six days a week. In the space below, write three journal entries. In the first entry, describe a typical hot summer day at the mill. In the second entry, describe a typical cold winter day at the mill. Include ideas about what you do at the mill, your working conditions, how the supervisor acts, and how you feel about your work. What do you see, hear, touch, and smell? In the third entry, describe what you do on a Sunday. Make more copies of this page or use your own paper if you need more room.

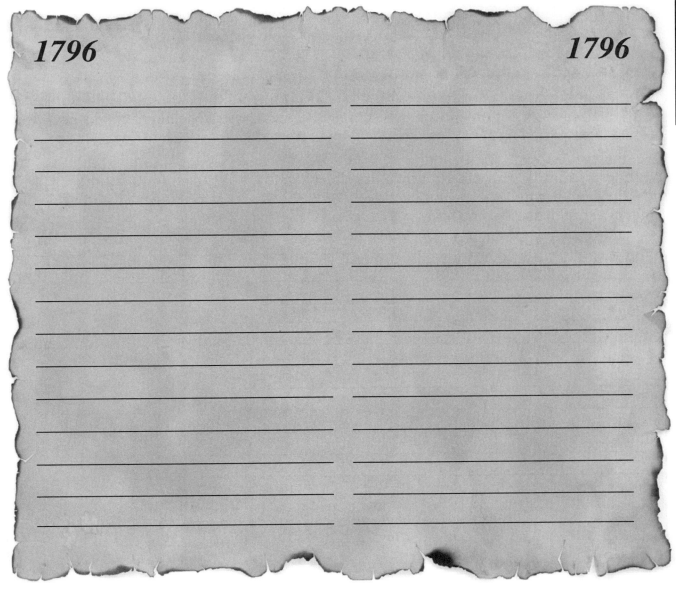

Name: _____   Date: _____

Meals, Now and Then

Have you ever thought about how easy it is to make breakfast? Answer each question below.

1. You pour a glass of cold milk. Did someone in your family
   _____ buy the milk at a store, or
   _____ milk a cow to get the milk?

2. You scramble some eggs. Did someone in your family
   _____ buy the eggs at a store, or
   _____ gather them from a chicken coop in your backyard?

3. You toast a slice of bread. Did someone in your family
   _____ buy the bread at a store, or
   _____ bake the loaf of bread from scratch?

4. You spread some jam on your toast. Did someone in your family
   _____ buy the jam at a store, or
   _____ make homemade jam?

There's a good chance that your family usually buys the items for meals at a store. Back in 1870, however, most Americans lived on farms or in small agricultural communities. They spent a large part of each day just preparing the food they needed for that day.

Graphic Organizer
Directions: Imagine that it is 1870, and that you need to prepare supper for your family. What would you have to do to prepare a supper of chicken, potatoes, pickles, bread, and apple pie? What preparations would you have had to make in advance? Describe your preparations in the box below. Then estimate how long you think these preparations would take.

FOOD/PREPARATION STEPS	PREPARATION TIME
chicken _____ _____ _____	_____
potatoes _____ _____ _____	_____
pickles _____ _____ _____	_____
bread _____ _____ _____	_____
apple pie _____ _____ _____	_____

UNIT ONE: INDUSTRIALIZATION

Name: _____ Date: _____

Preserving Food

In 1795, Napoleon Bonaparte offered a prize for anyone who could come up with a practical method of canning food. He wasn't interested in helping ordinary people find a convenient way to make meals. He just wanted a way to provide good food for his soldiers in battle.

Nicolas Appert, a French chef, discovered that he could put soups and stews or small fruits like raspberries and cherries into champagne bottles, seal them, and then plunge the bottles into boiling water. Appert did not understand why this process kept food fresh.

Two industrialists from Britain, John Hall and Bryan Donkin, became interested in Appert's work. They experimented and found that food could be better preserved by using cans made of tinplate sheet iron covered with a thin film of noncorrosive tin. By 1818, they were supplying tens of thousands of cans to the British navy.

At first, canned food was too costly for most people to buy. The food was very popular, however, with soldiers, sailors, and explorers because they could take an adequate supply of food with them wherever they went.

The United States was the first country to mass-produce food in cans in 1812. Canned goods slowly became affordable to most people. Women began to spend less time preparing food. They could create more interesting recipes. The canning industry also helped fishermen and farmers who supplied the food.

Vocabulary

Directions: As people learned how to preserve food, they experienced many emotions. Choose five words from those listed in the can on the right. Use each word in a sentence that explains why one of the people mentioned in the paragraphs above might have felt that way. An example is given.

Example: The women were *energized* because they spent less time preparing meals.

WORD BANK

eager	energized
confused	curious
excited	exhausted
relaxed	determined
freed	helpful
ambitious	creative

1. _____

_____

2. _____

3. _____

4. _____

5. _____

Name: _____ Date: _____

The First True Steam Engine

In the eighteenth century in England, engineers figured out a new way to power machines: steam. Steam power made industrialization grow by leaps and bounds.

How does steam power work? When water boils, the molecules expand with a tremendous force. As they turn to steam, they can fill a space nearly 2,000 times larger than the volume of the water. That's a lot of power!

Thomas Newcomen, an Englishman, put this power to work by inventing the first true steam engine in 1712. His engine was not very efficient, however. It could only be used for pumping water from coal mines.

Diagram

Directions: Look at the picture of Newcomen's engine. Write the correct word on each line from the list below.

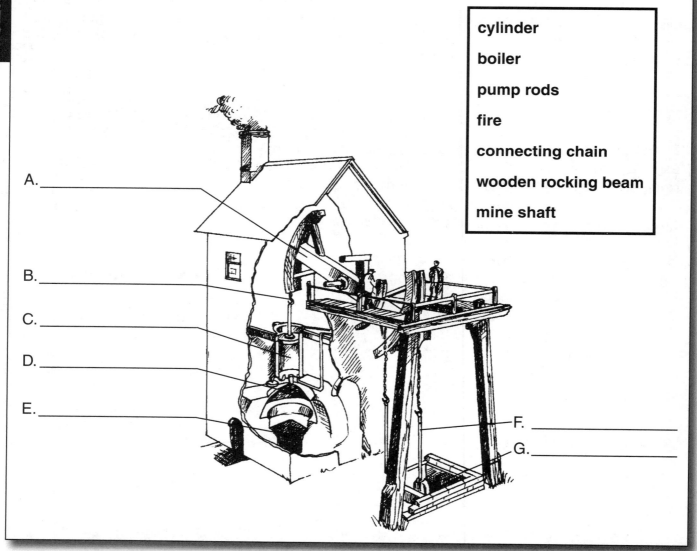

A. _____

B. _____

C. _____

D. _____

E. _____

F. _____

G. _____

cylinder
boiler
pump rods
fire
connecting chain
wooden rocking beam
mine shaft

Name: _____ Date: _____

James Watt Improves the Steam Engine

James Watt, from Scotland, greatly improved the Newcomen engine 50 years later. Then in 1782, Watt invented a steam engine that could produce **rotary motion**. That invention allowed steam engines to drive rotating shafts which, when connected with canvas belts, could power all kinds of machinery in paper, steel, and textile mills. A rotary engine could also drive the wheels of vehicles.

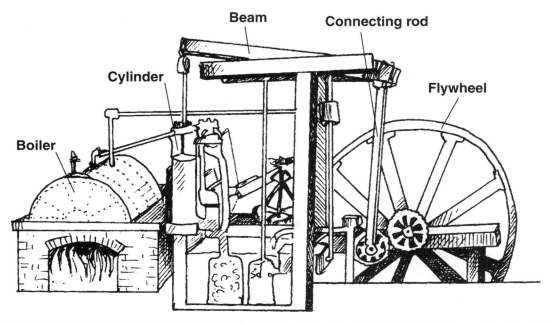

Research

Directions: Learn more about one of the topics below. Share your information with your classmates.

1. List five facts about Thomas Savery or the steam engine he invented.

2. Write a paragraph explaining how Newcomen's steam engine worked.

3. List five facts about Thomas Newcomen.

4. Draw a sketch of Thomas Newcomen's steam engine. Label the parts.

5. Write a paragraph explaining the improvements James Watt made to Newcomen's engine.

6. List five facts about the role Matthew Boulton had in the development of the steam engine.

7. Write a paragraph describing the first steam-driven vehicles.

8. List five fascinating facts about James Watt or his inventions.

9. Write a paragraph about the world's fastest steam car, the *Stanley Steamer Rocket.*

10. Find out why Newcomen's engine was inefficient.

Name: _____ Date: _____

Learning Steam Power Terms

Vocabulary

Directions: Define each of the following words using a dictionary. Draw a picture of *one* of the words in the picture frame below.

1. steam _____
   _____

2. condenser _____
   _____

3. boiler _____
   _____

4. engine _____
   _____

5. piston _____
   _____

6. rotary motion _____
   _____

7. governor _____
   _____

Name: _____ Date: _____

Water Power vs. Steam Power

Graphic Organizer

Directions: Read each question below. Then answer the question by checking the yes or no column.

	Yes	No
1. Would it be more time-consuming to grind wheat by a water-powered wheel than by hand?		
2. Since water-powered mills were usually built in the countryside, would it be easy to find enough workers?		
3. Would it be difficult to get raw materials to water-powered mills since streams that are good for power are usually not so good for transportation?		
4. Would it be difficult to get finished goods back to the cities from water-powered mills since streams that are good for power are usually not so good for transportation?		
5. Might streams and rivers freeze in the wintertime?		
6. Could a steam-powered factory be located in the middle of a city?		
7. Would it be difficult to find workers for a steam-powered factory in a city?		
8. Would a port city with good railroad connections and ship transportation be an ideal location for a steam-powered factory?		
9. Would it be difficult to transport raw materials to a steam-powered factory in a city?		
10. Would it be easy to transport finished goods from a steam-powered factory that was located in a city?		
11. Would New York and Philadelphia likely be among the first cities to become industrialized?		

UNIT ONE: INDUSTRIALIZATION

Robert Fulton

Robert Fulton, Jr., was born on a farm in Pennsylvania in 1765. He spent a happy childhood there until he was six years old. His mother particularly loved the farm's flower garden. Unfortunately, his father was not an experienced farmer. After several years of bad weather, the family was forced to sell the farm and move back to Lancaster where his father ran a successful tailoring shop. Two years later, Robert Fulton, Sr., became seriously ill and died.

Through his mother's hard work and the help of relatives, Robert was able to attend a private school. Although Fulton wasn't an outstanding student, he had a knack of looking at everyday tasks and finding new and interesting ways to complete them. When candles, which were in short supply, were forbidden at a Fourth of July celebration, he invented a successful skyrocket that he sent blazing upward. He also invented mechanical rowing paddles because he hated rowing the boat when he went fishing with his friends. He conducted many experiments with mercury at the time as well.

Fulton's other interest was painting and drawing. By the time he was 17, he had moved to Philadelphia where he sold some of his oil portraits, watercolor landscapes, and very small paintings called miniatures. He even made enough money to purchase a small farm for his mother in the countryside, complete with space for a flower garden.

Eventually, though, Fulton became quite ill. He went to Europe where he hoped to improve his health and become an even better painter. In Europe, however, there were many struggling painters like himself. Although he could support himself as an artist, he again became more interested in inventing things.

It was an exciting time to be in England because the Industrial Revolution was under-way. Everywhere he went in Europe, Fulton

studied new inventions and met with inventors. Fulton invented a machine to spin flax into linen and a device to twist hemp into rope. He also invented a machine that sawed large slabs of marble into smaller pieces. By 1797, he had even produced a design for a submarine.

Then Fulton met Robert R. Livingston, an American who was living in Europe. Mr. Livingston wanted to find a way to navigate New York's rivers by steamboat. He had the money to finance the project, and Fulton had the engineering ability. Fulton's first attempt at building the steamboat failed, so he had to start over again. By 1803, he had constructed a superior vehicle. He wanted to return to America, but he had to wait two years. The British government would not let anyone take a steam engine out of their country!

Finally, Fulton convinced the British to let him take a single steam engine to America. There he began working on a new steamboat that was 133 feet long and 18 feet wide. This steamboat, which was at first called the *North River Steamboat of Clermont* and later the *Clermont,* traveled about four miles an hour. That was a good speed in those days.

The steamboat traveled 150 miles on its first voyage in 1807 from New York City to Albany, the capital of New York state. Although he did not build the first steamboat, Fulton is credited with building the first commercially successful one.

Name: _____   Date: _____

Robert Fulton (cont.)

Directions: Complete the following activities.

UNIT ONE: INDUSTRIALIZATION

Fill in the Blanks

1. Fulton is credited with building the first commercially successful _____.

2. Fulton invented a machine to spin _____ into linen.

3. Fulton invented mechanical rowing _____ because he hated rowing the boat when he went fishing with his friends.

4. Fulton had a knack of looking at _____ tasks and finding new and interesting ways to complete them.

5. Robert R. Livingston _____ Fulton's steamboat project the *Clermont*.

True or False
Directions: Circle "T" for True or "F" for False.

1. T   F   Robert Fulton had been a successful artist as a young man.
2. T   F   Fulton studied art in Europe and met with artists while there.
3. T   F   Fulton's first attempt at building the steamboat failed.
4. T   F   Fulton invented a machine that sawed large logs into smaller pieces.
5. T   F   Robert Fulton got many of his ideas from his father who was a successful inventor.

Constructed Response

1. What two misfortunes happened to the Fulton family when Robert was young?

_____

_____

_____

2. List two reasons why Fulton became interested in inventing again.

_____

_____

_____

Critical Thinking

Why do you think the British government did not want steam engines to leave their country?

_____

_____

_____

Name: _____ Date: _____

Canals

Research

Directions: Using the Internet and other reference sources, work with a partner to answer the following questions. Use your own paper if you need more room.

1. What is a canal? _____
   _____

2. Why did people build canals? _____
   _____
   _____

3. What work did the horses and mules do along the canals? _____
   _____
   _____

4. Were mules or horses faster at pulling a barge? _____

5. Who were the hoggees? What did they do? _____
   _____
   _____

6. What type of work does a cobbler do? _____
   _____

7. Why might the hoggees need a cobbler? _____
   _____
   _____

8. What could happen to the canals and rivers in the wintertime? _____
   _____

9. Why was it easier to haul large loads by canals than
   by roads? _____
   _____
   _____
   _____

10. What is a lock on a canal?
    _____
    _____
    _____

DeWitt Clinton

The Erie Canal was the brainchild of DeWitt Clinton, who was born in 1769 in New York City. Clinton was educated at a private grammar school and at Columbia College, where he graduated at the head of his class. He was studying law when the American Constitution was under consideration by the states, and in 1787, he wrote a series of anonymous letters opposing ratification.

This placed him clearly in line with the beliefs of the Anti-Federalist Party—and also  brought him into continuous opposition during the administrations of Washington and Adams.

With the rise of this party as the Democratic-Republicans in 1801, Clinton became first a U.S. senator and then the mayor of New York City. Soon he was governor of the state, and in 1820, he was reelected to that position by only the narrowest of majorities.

While governor, Clinton proposed the idea of a canal connecting New York City with the West by a continuous waterway along the Hudson River up to Albany and by canal to Buffalo on Lake Erie. Clinton was not only the governor of the state but also head of the Canal Commission.

Finally, in 1817, the state legislature authorized construction of the project. It was, for that time, a mammoth project—some 363 miles (584 km) of canal construction and engineering. This meant, of course, that elevations had to be bypassed and that engineering techniques had to be developed to allow the canal to exist over valleys and rills. The last problem was solved by the construction of "water bridges" over transverse streams or depressed pockets of land. In other words, the water went over the bridge, rather than under it.

The depth of the canal was a little more than the size of an average man, and the motive power was provided by mules or horses. In the end, the cost seemed astronomical—$7,000,000—but in no time, the project brought returns many times that amount. Travel for passengers on the Erie Canal could be fairly comfortable and leisurely, since there was scarcely any water motion caused by the canal passage.

The long-range effect of the Erie Canal was that it began both a great wave of canal building throughout the country and a rapid speedup of immigration to the West. It reduced the cost of transport so much that it was possible for New York wheat to be sold more cheaply in Savanna, Georgia, than the homegrown wheat brought from Georgia's interior.

After all of this, one would think that DeWitt Clinton would become the toast of the nation, but it was not to be. He had made enemies during his life, and they helped bring an end to his fruitful political career. He died in 1828.

Did You Know?
Men working on the canal boats were separated from their families on shore for long periods of time. Others chose to take their families with them on the canals. In 1921, 354 children were found living on canal boats with their families.

Name: _____ Date: _____

DeWitt Clinton (cont.)

Directions: Complete the following activities.

Fill in the Blanks

1. DeWitt Clinton proposed the idea of a canal connecting New York City with the _____.

2. The Erie Canal is _____ miles long.

3. The Erie Canal created a continuous waterway from the _____ _____ to Lake Erie.

4. Clinton became first a U.S. _____, then _____ of New York City, and then a two-term _____ of the state of New York.

5. The Erie Canal cost _____ to build.

Time Line

Directions: Number the events in order from 1 (first) to 4 (last). Use the reading exercise about DeWitt Clinton for reference.

_____ A. The New York state legislature authorized construction of the Erie Canal.
_____ B. DeWitt Clinton wrote a series of anonymous letters opposing the ratification of the U.S. Constitution.
_____ C. DeWitt Clinton was born in New York City.
_____ D. Clinton was reelected governor of New York.

Cause and Effect

Directions: A cause is an event that produces a result. An effect is the result produced. Write three effects for the cause listed below.

Cause: The Erie Canal was built.

Effect #1: _____

_____

Effect #2: _____

_____

Effect #3: _____

_____

Name: _____   Date: _____

The Erie Canal

The most famous canal in America was the Erie Canal. Work began on this canal in 1817. By 1825, it was finished. The canal covered a distance of 363 miles (584 km). It connected New York City with the Great Lakes via the Hudson River.

Look at the map below.

1. Use an atlas to find the names of the following cities on the map: New York City, Albany, Utica, Syracuse, Rochester, and Buffalo. Write the names in the appropriate places.

2. Label the Hudson River, the Atlantic Ocean, Lake Erie, and Lake Ontario.

3. Draw in the route of the Erie Canal.

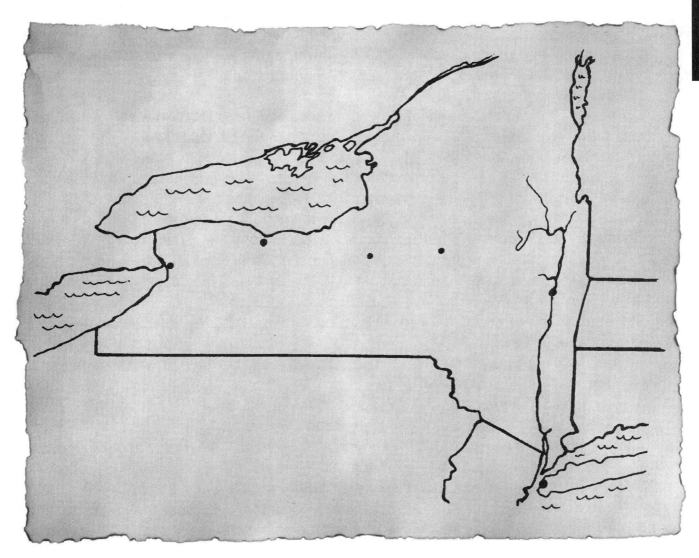

UNIT ONE: INDUSTRIALIZATION

Name: _____   Date: _____

Fascinating Facts About the Erie Canal

Research

Directions: Learn more about the Erie Canal. Use your research to fill in the blanks with words from the box.

farmers	Buffalo	cities	Ireland	tolls
one dollar	freight	1817	eastern	mills
85	hostellers	deep	wide	thousands
hoggees	Lake Erie	west	immigration	steam trains

1. Construction on the Erie Canal began in Rome, New York, on July 4, _____.
2. Parts of the canal were built by wealthy _____ along the canal route.
3. Many immigrants from _____ helped build the canal.
4. The laborers received eighty cents to _____ per day for their work.
5. There were _____ locks along the Erie Canal.
6. When the canal was completed in 1825, the governor of New York, DeWitt Clinton, sailed from Buffalo to New York City. There, he emptied a barrel of _____ water into the Atlantic Ocean!
7. Farmers started farms throughout the Great Lakes and the Upper Midwest. They shipped their farm products to the _____ part of the United States.
8. The canal helped create many large _____ along its route.
9. _____ were built near the canal. Nearby rivers and streams provided water power. Goods were shipped quickly and cheaply along the canal.
10. The canal encouraged _____ to the Great Lakes area.
11. Consumer goods were shipped _____ along the canal.
12. _____ was shipped along the canal at about 55 miles per 24 hours.
13. People could travel faster than freight along the canal. It only took passengers about four days to travel from New York City to _____.
14. At first, the canal was only four feet (1.2 m) _____. Later, it was deepened to seven feet (2.1 m).
15. At first, the canal was 40 feet (12.2 m) _____. Later it was widened to 70 feet (21.3 m).
16. At first, people had to pay _____ to use the canal.
17. By 1845, _____ of boats used the Erie Canal.
18. A typical crew on a boat included the captain, the steersman, the cook, the deckhand, and the _____. Thousands of people found work as lock tenders, toll collectors, bridge operators, surveyors, repair crews, and bank patrollers.
19. Many merchants, _____, and shopkeepers lived near the canals to feed, clothe, house, and supply the people who worked on the canals.
20. By the 1850s, people were shipping goods by _____ instead of by canals.

Name: _____ Date: _____

Traveling on the Erie Canal

Journaling

Directions: Imagine that you are traveling along the Erie Canal from Buffalo to Albany in 1840. Use the information from the fascinating facts on the previous page to write a journal entry. Describe what you see, hear, taste, touch, and smell along the way.

1840   *1840*

_____   _____

_____   _____

_____   _____

_____   _____

_____   _____

_____   _____

_____   _____

_____   _____

_____   _____

_____   _____

_____   _____

_____   _____

_____   _____

Name: _____ Date: _____

Low Bridge

The Erie Canal even has a well-known song associated with it. It is called the "Erie Canal Song," but it is also known as "Low Bridge." It was published in 1913 to protest the coming of the mechanized barge.

Directions: Find the music to this song. Practice singing it with your classmates. If you can play a musical instrument, learn the music and accompany the singers.

The "Erie Canal Song" or "Low Bridge"

1. I've got an old mule and her name is Sal
Fifteen miles on the Erie Canal
She's a good old worker and a good old pal
Fifteen miles on the Erie Canal.

2. We've hauled some barges in our day
Filled with lumber, coal, and hay
And every inch of the way we know
From Albany to Buffalo.

3. Low bridge, everybody down
Low bridge for we're coming to a town
And you'll always know your neighbor
And you'll always know your pal
If you've ever navigated on
The Erie Canal.

4. We'd better get along on our way, old gal
Fifteen miles on the Erie Canal
'Cause you bet your life I'd never part with Sal
Fifteen miles on the Erie Canal.

5. Git up there mule, here comes a lock
We'll make Rome 'bout six o'clock
One more trip and back we'll go
Right back home to Buffalo.

6. Low bridge, everybody down
Low bridge for we're coming to a town
And you'll always know your neighbor
And you'll always know your pal
If you've ever navigated on
The Erie Canal.

Lockport on the Erie Canal by W.H. Bartlett, 1839

All About Iron

Cooperative Learning

Directions: Work with a partner to answer the following questions. Use the Internet and other reference sources if you need help.

1. What do you think people made tools out of before they had iron?

   _____

   _____

2. What would be the problem with these kinds of materials?

   _____

   _____

3. During the Iron Age, which was about 3,500 years ago, the Hittites learned how to make tools out of iron. What advantage would iron tools have over the previous kinds of tools?

   _____

   _____

4. Iron was an ideal metal because it could be melted, shaped, hammered, and cast. However, it was very difficult to get the iron out of the iron ore. What is iron ore?

   _____

   _____

5. The blast furnace was first invented during the Middle Ages. A blast furnace was a huge stone oven in which charcoal, iron ore, and limestone were burned. The charcoal became very hot and made carbon monoxide. It reacted chemically with the iron ore to separate out the impurities from the metal. What pure metal was left?

   _____

6. In the late 1700s, Abraham Darby III built the first iron bridge across the River Severn in England. It is still there today. He showed that iron was an ideal material for building large structures. What else besides bridges would benefit from an iron framework?

   _____

   _____

7. Why would an iron-framed building be ideal for a textile mill?

   _____

   _____

   _____

Name: _____ Date: _____

Taller and Taller Buildings

Internet Scavenger Hunt
Directions: Using key words or phrases from each question, search the Internet to find the answers.

1. Cast iron began to be used for buildings as well as bridges. In 1851, the Great Exhibition was held in London. The exhibit hall had 300,000 panes of glass in a huge iron frame that covered 2,000 acres (809.4 hectares) and held eight miles (12.87 km) of display tables. The exhibition showed how far-reaching industrialism had become in Britain.

   What was the name of the exhibit hall? _____

2. For the Paris Exhibition of 1889, a famous iron building was constructed.

   What is the name of this tower that is still standing in Paris? _____

3. After a while, cast iron was replaced by rolled steel. Architects in the United States started to use steel frames. The first skyscraper in America was built in 1885 in Chicago.

   What was the name of this ten-story-high building? _____

4. Architects next began to use reinforced concrete, which is liquid concrete poured over steel rods. The first large skyscraper made of steel and concrete was the Woolworth Building in New York City in 1913. It was 794 feet high (242 meters).

   How many stories did this building have? _____

5. Architects continued to build skyscrapers in America because of the shortage of land in cities. In 1931, the Empire State Building was opened in New York.

   How tall is this building? _____

6. In 1974, the Sears Tower opened in Chicago.

   How tall is this building, now called the Willis Tower?

   _____

7. How tall is the CN Tower in Toronto, Canada? _____

8. How tall are the Petronas Towers in Kuala Lumpur in Malaysia?

   _____

9. How tall is the Burj Khalifa in Dubai, United Arab Emirates?

   _____

   How many stories does this building have? _____

Name: _____   Date: _____

Inventing a Safe Elevator

Fill in the Blanks

Directions: Read the story below about the invention of the elevator. Fill in the blanks with words from the box.

mass-produced	possible	stairs	hoists
standard-sized	World's Fair	elevator	cut
safety mechanism	New York City	cables	Otis

In 1847, James Bogardus built a five-story factory in (1) _____ made out of cast iron. He also built other factories using (2) _____ parts. These were the first (3) _____ buildings.

As buildings got higher, goods were brought up from floor to floor by mechanical (4) _____. Sometimes the (5) _____ on these hoists broke, so people did not want to use them. Understandably, they also did not want to climb up flight after flight of (6) _____.

This problem was solved by Elisha (7) _____,
who was an engineer from Vermont. He invented a
(8) _____ to hold the hoist in
place even if the cables slipped or broke. He used a series
of vertical pieces to grab the (9) _____
in case of an accident. Otis showed the public at the
(10) _____ in 1853 that his invention was
safe. He got into an elevator, which was then lifted high up
into the air. The cables were then (11) _____,
but the elevator did not crash.

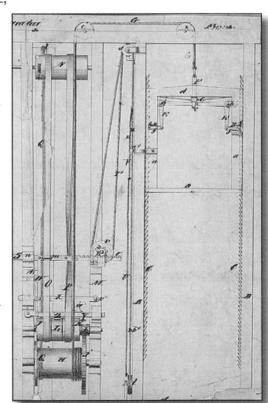

By 1857, the first safety elevator was installed in a New York City department store. Today's skyscrapers would not be (12) _____ if the elevator had not been invented.

UNIT ONE: INDUSTRIALIZATION

Name: _____ Date: _____

How Did Steam Locomotives Affect America?

Directions: Many changes took place as railroads were built and steam locomotives began to cross America. Read each statement below. If you think the statement tells about a change that was at least partly due to the railroads or steam locomotives, put a plus sign (+) on the line. If you think the statement tells about a change that was not due to the railroads or steam locomotives, put a minus sign (-) on the line. The first one is done for you.

__+__ 1. People began to ship fewer goods by canals.

_____ 2. It was easier to transport goods and people to the interior part of America.

_____ 3. More iron and steel were produced.

_____ 4. More coal was produced.

_____ 5. Big cities and little towns were connected via the railroads.

_____ 6. It was easier to transport coal to factories.

_____ 7. Business became nationwide.

_____ 8. More Americans and European immigrants settled land in the interior part of America.

_____ 9. Farmers could transport agricultural products to new markets.

_____ 10. New towns were set up along the railroads.

_____ 11. Ranchers could transport their cattle to markets.

_____ 12. More telegraph lines were set up.

_____ 13. Many people found jobs laying track.

_____ 14. Air pollution increased.

_____ 15. More raw materials and finished goods were transported from one region to another.

_____ 16. The western part of the country was linked to the eastern part of the country.

Critical Thinking

Directions: Choose one of the statements above. In a short paragraph, explain how the railroads and steam locomotives helped to bring about that change. Give specific details or examples to support your opinion.

_____

_____

_____

_____

_____

Samuel Morse

You may already know that Samuel Morse invented the telegraph. You probably also realize that the idea for a telegraph just didn't "spring out" of his head one day. He had to study in school and get some experience inventing things. His knowledge and experience were two of the "ingredients" that helped him become an inventor.

Samuel Morse was born in 1791. He disliked school except for his interest in electricity and art. Although his parents could barely afford it, they sent Samuel to London to study art. In time, he became an excellent painter. He returned to America, hoping to paint portraits of Americans for a living. It was difficult to find customers, so he had to travel from town to town. In 1818, he married Lucretia Pickering, and they eventually had three children.

Samuel had a difficult time supporting his family as an artist. He tried to make money by doing other things, such as inventing a water pump for firefighters and a marble-cutting machine. Although neither idea was a success, he gained experience inventing things.

Samuel's wife died in 1825 of heart trouble. Sadly, Samuel placed his children with family members, and then he returned to Europe for more training as an artist. His dream was to be chosen as one of the artists who would paint a mural in the rotunda of the U. S. Capitol.

While he was in France, he learned about the semaphore telegraph system. In this system, tall platforms, or **semaphores**, were placed about 15 miles apart from each other. A man stood at the top of each semaphore and held up a huge code for the next person to see. Then the message was repeated to the next semaphore. Of course, this system didn't work on foggy days. Morse's knowledge about the semaphore system helped him think about how messages could be sent over long distances.

On the ship home from Europe, Samuel heard the passengers talking about electricity. He already had an interest in electricity, experience as an inventor, and knowledge about the semaphore system. Now he had an inspiration—a new idea—that electricity might be able to transmit messages. He developed a simple electric telegraph system on the trip home.

Samuel Morse was practical. He didn't need fancy materials for his invention. He used an ordinary picture frame, a table, and a piece of lead that he melted and molded. His system was simple, and it worked!

Everyone ignored Samuel's invention. He needed money, so he became a professor of painting and sculpture at the University of the City of New York. When he learned that his dream to paint a mural in the rotunda had fallen through, he never painted seriously again.

He started to work on the telegraph once more. He had to make his own supplies, including buying wire in pieces, joining it together, and insulating it with cotton. In 1837, he strung ten miles of wire around his classroom, and then invited wealthy businessmen in for a demonstration. After that, Samuel formed a partnership with two other men, and together they continued to improve the telegraph.

Did You Know?
The need for the Pony Express ended when telegraph wires were strung across the country.

UNIT ONE: INDUSTRIALIZATION

Name: _____ Date: _____

Morse Code

A telegraph works by allowing signals to be sent along a wire. At first, telegraphs were used by the railroads to keep track of trains. Later, telegraph cables linked major cities. Today, Morse code, the system of signals devised by Morse, has been largely replaced by modern communication systems. Morse code is mainly used by amateur radio operators all around the world.

Morse code uses a system of signals to send messages. The signals are made up of short dots (short electric pulses) and long dashes (longer electric pulses) that represent the letters of the alphabet and the numerals 0 through 9.

Decoding

Directions: Study the code below, and then figure out each of the messages. Then, on your own sheet of paper, write a message for a friend using Morse code. Use three spaces between letters and six spaces between words.

A	• —	H	• • • •	O	— — —	U	• • —
B	— • • •	I	• •	P	• — — •	V	• • • —
C	— • — •	J	• — — —	Q	— — • —	W	• — —
D	— • •	K	— • —	R	• — •	X	— • • —
E	•	L	• — • •	S	• • •	Y	— • — —
F	• • — •	M	— —	T	—	Z	— — • •
G	— — •	N	— •				

UNIT ONE: INDUSTRIALIZATION

1. What does the message say?

   • • •   — — —   • • •

   ____   ____   ____

2. What does the message say?

   — — •   — — —   — — —   — • •   — • • •   — • — —   •

   ____   ____   ____   ____   ____   ____   ____

Name: _____   Date: _____

Alike and Different

Graphic Organizer

Directions: Learn more about Samuel Morse and Robert Fulton. How were Samuel Morse and Robert Fulton alike? How were they different from each other? Look at the words and phrases below. Which ones apply only to Samuel Morse? Which ones apply only to Robert Fulton? Which words or phrases apply to both men? Fill in the boxes below to show how these men were alike and how they were different from one another.

Robert Fulton

Samuel Morse

Persevered	**Experienced hardships**	**Born in 1765**
Invented several things	**Wanted to be a painter**	**Born in 1791**
Studied art in Europe	**Early interest in electricity**	

Early interest in finding new ways to complete tasks

SAMUEL MORSE	BOTH MEN	ROBERT FULTON

Disappointment and Perseverance

So many of the inventors that you have read about experienced disappointments in their lives. For example, Samuel Morse was an excellent painter, but he had a difficult time supporting his family as an artist. He tried to paint portraits for a living, but it was difficult to find customers. He had to travel from town to town looking for work. He also studied art in Europe in the hopes that he would be selected as one of the painters for a mural in the rotunda of the U.S. Capitol. It was a huge disappointment for him when he was not selected.

Critical Thinking

Directions: Give specific details or examples to support your answers to the following questions.

1. Why do you think inventors like Morse succeeded in spite of the disappointments in their lives?

    _____

    _____

    _____

2. Most everyone experiences some disappointment in his or her life. What disappointment have you or someone you know experienced?

    _____

    _____

    _____

    _____

3. Did that disappointment help you or someone you know in some way?

    _____

    _____

    _____

4. Many of the inventors that you read about persevered. They didn't give up in spite of the fact that they had failures along the way. Robert Fulton's first steamboat, for example, sank and splintered into pieces. In the long run, however, the inventors' perseverance paid off. In what ways have you or someone you know persevered? How did your perseverance pay off in the long run?

    _____

    _____

    _____

    _____

    _____

UNIT ONE: INDUSTRIALIZATION

Name: _____   Date: _____

A History of Electricity

Directions: Read each paragraph. Find the sentence in each paragraph that does not belong there. Cross it out.

1. Throughout most of history, people did not know much about electricity. At first, people only knew about electricity in the form of lightning. Lightning frightened many people. The ancient Greeks discovered that rubbing amber, a fossilized gum from trees, made it attract objects such as feathers or straw. That was what we now call static electricity.

2. In the 1600s, scientists in Europe began to experiment with electricity. They realized that a machine in which a piece of cloth was rubbed continuously against a glass plate would produce a flow or current of electricity. Then Pieter van Musschenbroek, a professor of physics at Leyden University in the Netherlands, realized that an electric current could be stored for a brief time in a jar of water. The Netherlands is a small country in Europe. The spark from it could give an electric shock. His device was called the Leyden jar.

3. In America, Benjamin Franklin first proved that lightning was a form of electricity. During a thunderstorm in 1752, he flew a kite that had a key tied to the end of the string. When lightning hit the kite, a current of static electricity flowed down the string into the key and then onto the ground. That caused a series of sparks. When Franklin connected the kite to a Leyden jar, the water in the jar became electrically charged. Those sparks were amazing. Franklin figured out that the sparks were caused by negative and positive charges being brought together.

4. In 1800, an Italian professor, Alessandro Volta, invented several devices for storing electricity. Electricity was an interesting subject. Then in 1820, a Danish scientist named Hans Christian Oersted discovered the link between magnetism and electricity. When Oersted placed a compass near a wire carrying an electric current, the needle in the compass moved. He realized that electrical energy could be converted into mechanical energy. Electricity could make things move!

5. In 1821, an English scientist, Michael Faraday, showed that electricity could produce rotary motion. He also made the first electric dynamo in 1831. Practical generators were not available, though, until the 1870s. I wonder why it took so long.

6. In 1879, Thomas Edison made improvements to the electric light bulb. Edison also invented the phonograph. Because the light bulbs were safe to use in homes, everyone wanted to have electric power. Edison figured out how to mass-produce lights. He developed supply systems and built the first power station in 1881. Electric power began to replace steam power.

Name: _____ Date: _____

Learning Electricity Terms

Matching

Directions: Match each word to its definition. Use the Internet and other reference sources if you need help.

_____ 1. A piece of equipment that changes the voltage of an electric current.

_____ 2. This word is the shortened form of dynamoelectric. It is another name for a generator.

_____ 3. A place that houses the dynamo or generator.

_____ 4. An engine that is driven by water, steam, or gas passing through the blades of a wheel and making it revolve.

_____ 5. A form of energy caused by the motion of electrons and protons. It can be produced by rotating a magnet within a coil of wire.

_____ 6. A machine that provides the power to make something run or work.

_____ 7. A machine that produces electricity by turning a magnet inside a coil of wire.

_____ 8. The movement of electricity through a wire.

a. Electricity

b. Motor

c. Turbine

d. Electric current

e. Transformer

f. Dynamo

g. Power station

h. Generator

Name: _____ Date: _____

How Does Electricity Affect the Earth?

Fill in the Blanks

Directions: Fill in the sentences using the words in the box below. You will not need all the words.

space	temperature	steam	heat	fossil
decreasing	greenhouse	increasing	magic	oxygen
generators	coal	reduce	renewable	energy
water	turbines	nuclear	iron	waves
carbon dioxide				

1. Electricity requires energy, which is produced by burning ___ ___ ___◯

2. The coal heats the water and turns it into __◯_ ___ ___ ___.

3. The steam powers the turbines, which drive the electric ___ ___ ___ ___ ___ ◯___ ___ ___.

4. Burning coal produces a gas called ___ ___ ___ ___ ___ ___ ◯___ ___ ___ ___ ___.

5. The amount of carbon dioxide in the air is ___ ___ ___◯___ ___ ___ ___ ___.

6. The sun's heat reaches the earth. The carbon dioxide traps the ___◯___ ___ that is radiated back from the earth's surface.

7. The heat does not escape into space. This is called the ___ ___◯___ ___ ___ ___ ___ ___ ___ effect. This may cause the earth's temperature to rise quickly.

8. Many nations are trying to ___ ___ ___ ___◯___ the amount of carbon dioxide that they produce.

9. Coal, gas, and oil are called ___ ___ ___ ___◯___ fuels. They will eventually be used up.

10. Some ___ ___ ___ ___ ___◯ sources do not get used up. They are called renewable sources of energy.

11. ___ ___◯___ ___ ___ ___ energy might work if the risks of accidents could be lessened.

12. Write the letters in circles here: ___ ___ ___ ___ ___ ___ ___ ___ ___ ___ ___ ___

13. Unscramble the circled letters and write the word on the line. _____

Thomas Alva Edison

Thomas Alva Edison was America's leading inventor of the nineteenth century. He was born in Milan, Ohio, in 1847. His father, Samuel Edison, was a shingle manufacturer at that time. Shortly thereafter, however, the family moved to Port Huron, Michigan, where Samuel ran a grain and lumber business.

As a boy, Tom Edison lost much of his hearing, and his formal schooling was fragmentary. He didn't do well in school, so his mother took him out of school and taught him herself. Tom hated mathematics, but was fascinated by chemistry.

During his early teens, Tom read voraciously and studied the art of sending and receiving telegraphic messages. He got a job as a telegraph operator. He worked the night shift, which left him plenty of time to read and experiment. He learned to stay awake for long periods of time.

In 1868, while working for the Western Union Telegraph Company in Boston, Edison took out his first patent—for an electrographic vote recorder. In the following year, he patented the stock ticker. From money earned in various enterprises, Edison then set up an "invention factory"—a sort of research laboratory for new devices.

He soon acquired patents in rapid succession. He devised a means of creating quadruplex telegraphy (sending several messages at the same time over the same cable). He improved on Alexander Graham Bell's telephone by developing a carbon transmitter.

In 1878, after he moved his laboratory to Menlo Park, New Jersey, he produced the phonograph and followed that fantastic creation with patents for improvement of the device.

Edison did not invent the incandescent lamp, but he did make a reliable one. Experiments on the electric light had been carried on in England in the 1840s, but Edison perfected the blend between a carbon filament and the vacuum bulb in 1879, thus paving the way for the first electric lighting system in New York in 1882.

Edison did not invent the first successful movie projector—Thomas Armat did—but Edison bought the patent for it and actually began the movie industry in 1908.

There are many interesting facets to Edison's life. He invented the vacuum tube, necessary to early radio, but he could see no immediate value to the device and ended his work on it. He worked on the storage battery, the dictating machine, and the mimeograph prior to World War I. During the war, he conducted research upon torpedoes, flame throwers, and periscopes.

He also worked with Henry Ford and Harvey Firestone on a project to produce rubber from domestic plants—a project that was revived in World War II.

Edison was a practical inventor. He created items that were immediately useful in the home or in business. He was, in a way, a genius, and yet, as he stated, his inventions came from "one percent inspiration and ninety-nine percent perspiration." He did work 20 hours out of almost every day in his adult life.

Name: _____ Date: _____

Thomas Alva Edison (cont.)

Time Line Activity

Directions: Number the events in order from 1 (first) to 10 (last). Use the reading exercise for reference.

_____ A.   Bought the patent for the movie projector and began the movie industry.

_____ B.   Invented the vacuum tube, necessary to early radio.

_____ C.   In 1868, Edison took out his first patent—for an electrographic vote recorder.

_____ D.   In 1882, the first electric lighting system in New York was installed.

_____ E.   Edison devised the means of creating quadruplex telegraphy.

_____ F.   During World War I, he conducted research upon torpedoes, flame throwers, and periscopes.

_____ G.   He improved on Bell's telephone by developing a carbon transmitter.

_____ H.   Edison was born in Milan, Ohio, in 1847.

_____ I.   Edison set up an invention factory.

_____ J.   He invented the phonograph.

True or False

Directions: Circle "T" for True or "F" for False.

1. T   F   Edison invented the incandescent lamp.

2. T   F   Edison invented the first successful movie projector.

3. T   F   Edison invented the stock ticker.

4. T   F   Edison did not invent the phonograph.

5. T   F   Edison did not invent the telegraph.

Name: _____ Date: _____

Thomas Edison Crossword Puzzle

Directions: Use the clues below to complete the crossword puzzle. You may need to do some research on the Internet or with other reference sources.

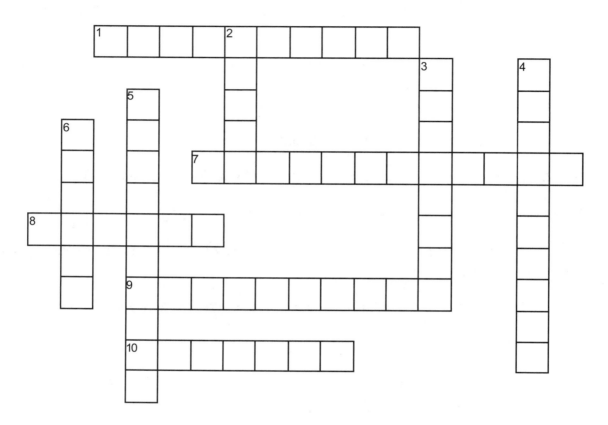

ACROSS

1. Edison built the world's first power station in 1881. The Pearl Street Station relied on steam from burning coal to power the _____.

7. Thomas Edison said, "Genius is one percent inspiration and ninety-nine percent _____."

8. Thomas Edison was the most _____ inventor of his day.

9. When Edison was asked about his _____, he said, "I'll retire the day before my funeral."

10. During his lifetime, Edison registered 1,093 _____.

DOWN

2. The first phonograph recording was the nursery _____, "Mary Had a Little Lamb."

3. In 1879, Edison perfected the electric _____ lamp, which burned for 45 hours.

4. When Thomas Edison was ten years old, he set up his own _____ at home.

5. Edison's favorite invention was the _____.

6. People were so amazed by the phonograph that Edison was called "The _____ of Menlo Park."

Name: _____   Date: _____

One Thing Affects Another

Cause and Effect

Directions: During industrialization, a change in one area often brought about changes in other areas. A **cause** is an event that produces a result. An **effect** is the result produced. Read each section below and fill in the cause or the effect.

1. Steam-powered factories needed a lot of coal to heat the boilers. As a result, the coal industry boomed.

    Cause: Steam-powered factories needed a lot of coal to heat the boilers.

    Effect: _____

2. The coal industry, however, needed trains with powerful engines and strong rails made of high-quality steel to bring the coal to the factories. Fortunately, at that same time, a technology that allowed the production of large quantities of high-quality steel came along. Therefore, many railroads were built in the United States.

    Cause: _____

    _____

    Effect: Many railroads were built in the United States.

3. Because of all the new railroads, the mail delivery was speeded up.

    Cause: _____

    Effect: _____

4. The invention of the telegraph by Samuel Morse speeded up communication even more. Americans could quickly find out prices from distant cities and place orders. The quick exchange of information also allowed newspapers to report news from across the nation. Even railroad engineers used the telegraph to find out exactly where the trains were at any moment.

    Cause: The telegraph speeded up communication even more.

    Effect #1: _____

    Effect #2: _____

    Effect #3: _____

Name: _____   Date: _____

Get the Message?

Critical Thinking

Directions: Read the information, do some research, and answer the questions. Use your own paper if you need more room.

1. A long time ago, North American Plains Indians used smoke signals to send messages. What types of messages do you think might have been sent by smoke signals?

_____

2. By 1830, people knew about batteries. They realized that if they just had very long wires, they could send electric signals over long distances. Then Samuel Morse invented the telegraph, and in 1844, he sent the first long-distance message. What were his words?

_____

3. By 1852, there were telegraph lines all across North America and Europe. By 1866, a telegraph cable crossed the Atlantic Ocean! If you had been the first to send a message across the ocean, what would it have said?

_____

4. Next, inventors wanted to figure out how to change the pattern of someone's voice into electrical signals. Alexander Graham Bell did just that in 1876 when he invented a simple machine that changed sound to electrical signals. The first words that he spoke on the telephone were an accident. He had just spilled some acid in his workroom, so he called for help on his test system to his assistant Thomas Watson, who was in the next room. If you had invented the telephone and wanted your words to be memorable, what would you have said?

_____

_____

5. In 1901, Guglielmo Marconi sent radio messages across the Atlantic Ocean from England to North America. What message would you have sent?

_____

_____

6. In 1969, Neil Armstrong sent a message from the moon to the earth. What did his message say?

_____

Name: _____   Date: _____

Hello, How Are You?

How do you call a friend on a traditional land-line telephone? You pick up the phone and key in the number. What happens when your friend answers the telephone and says "Hello?" What happens when you speak into the mouthpiece of a traditional household phone?

The sound of your voice makes a flat piece of metal in the mouthpiece vibrate. That stretches and squashes tiny carbon granules that are stored in a container of the mouthpiece. Electricity travels through those carbon granules, allowing the sound of your voice to be converted into fast-changing electrical pulses or signals.

Your friend can hear your voice because the signals have traveled along the wires to the earpiece of his or her telephone. The signals pass through a wire coil that is called an electromagnet. That produces magnetism that pulls on a sheet of metal in the earpiece. The strength of the magnetism varies with the fast-changing signals, making the metal move back and forth very quickly. These are the sound waves that your friend hears.

Diagram

Directions: After reading the paragraphs above about how a telephone works, number the statements below in the correct sequence.

A. _____ A flat piece of metal in the mouthpiece vibrates.

B. _____ The metal in the earpiece moves back and forth quickly.

C. _____ Your friend answers the telephone.

D. _____ The signals pass through an electromagnet.

E. _____ The signals travel along the wires to the earpiece of your friend's telephone.

F. _____ The magnetism pulls on a sheet of metal in the earpiece.

G. _____ Your voice is converted into fast-changing electrical sounds and pulses.

H. _____ Electricity travels through the carbon granules.

I. _____ You call a friend.

J. _____ Tiny carbon granules are stretched and squashed in a container of the mouthpiece.

K. _____ The strength of the magnetism varies with the fast-changing signals.

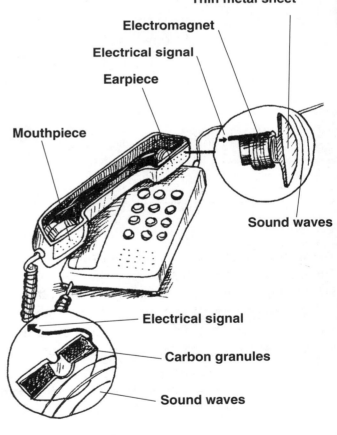

Thin metal sheet

Electromagnet

Electrical signal

Earpiece

Mouthpiece

Sound waves

Electrical signal

Carbon granules

Sound waves

Name: _____ Date: _____

Into the Air!

If you have ever taken an airplane flight, you know that it is usually a smooth ride. You can sit in your seat watching television or listening to music. An attendant serves you a snack or a meal. In a few hours, you can travel thousands of miles.

It wasn't like that on the first flight back in 1903. On that flight, Orville Wright had to lie on his stomach between the wings of a machine that looked like an oversized kite. The flight lasted just 12 seconds and covered only 120 feet. After the *Flyer* landed, a gust of wind caught it and wrecked it! Still, Orville Wright was the first person to make a powered flight in a heavier-than-air machine. Orville and his brother Wilbur didn't give up, though. By 1906, they had built an airplane that could stay in the air for 38 minutes and cover nearly 25 miles.

Many European governments became interested in flying. In 1914, at the start of World War I, pilots first used aircraft to check enemy positions. Later, planes were used for aerial combat and to bomb troops and civilians. After the war, pilots set up the first airmail and passenger services.

Many metal-framed bombers were built and used in World War II. After the war ended in 1945, airlines set up passenger services criss-crossing the world. Airplanes were also used to take injured people to hospitals; to deliver urgently needed medicine, food, and supplies; and to help farmers with their crops.

Although Wilbur Wright died suddenly in 1912, Orville Wright lived until 1948. Think of all the changes in aviation he experienced during his lifetime!

Research

Directions: Choose 10 events from the history of flight. Create an illustrated time line. Cut a piece of yarn two meters long. Place the date of the event on a plain 3″ x 5″ index card. On the front of the index card, draw a picture of the event and write one sentence describing it. Punch a hole in the top of the card and tie it to your yarn time line in the appropriate place. Repeat this procedure with the other events. Put the cards in chronological order, and leave enough string on both ends to allow you to display your time line.

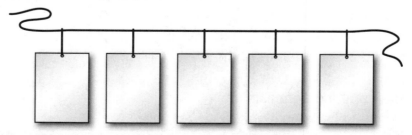

Henry Ford and the Assembly Line

The assembly-line process used to produce the famous Model T Ford was one of America's great gifts to the world. However, Henry Ford did not discover the idea of an assembly line.

The notion of interchangeable parts goes back to the manufacture of muskets for the U.S. Army in 1798. Congress, anxious to outfit its newly created army, began to let contracts for the acquisition of guns. One of the first of these went to Eli Whitney, a New England inventor who had become famous, though not rich, from his previous invention of the cotton gin. Whitney was given a contract to provide some 10,000 muskets, a considerable number of guns for that time in America.

Whitney realized immediately that to make such a quantity of weapons through the old method of making each part for each weapon would take too long. Se he decided to take a revolutionary course. He decided to make the parts of the muskets identical, so as the musket was passed down the table, the workmen would reach into a pile of such parts and place one of each in each gun. This was the beginning of what came to be known as the **assembly-line process**.

In was not entirely a new idea. Thomas Jefferson had thought of such a method earlier, but Whitney was the first to demonstrate the effectiveness of the idea. Whitney's greatest difficulty was in getting the exact **duplication** of parts. Today, when the batteries of your flashlight go dead, you can immediately buy some more of an exact size and fit. In 1800, the methods of precision manufacturing were not present, and Whitney had frequent setbacks in the production of his muskets.

The assembly-line concept existed in American industry during the remainder of Whitney's century, but it was not common. Finally, after 1900, the age of the automobile

was to bring the assembly line to complete reality. Henry Ford was the person most responsible for making the change possible.

Ford organized his company to manufacture automobiles in 1903. After indifferent success, he decided in 1909 to concentrate on the production of the Model T. He simplified the design and produced the car by the assembly-line process. By doing so, he reduced the price of his auto from $950 in 1909 to $290 in 1924.

The Model T was high and boxlike in design. It had only a hand throttle, plus one forward gear and a reverse. Ford eliminated the rear door, only painting a line to indicate where a door might have been. Since each Model T had a canvas top, it didn't make much difference anyway. The passengers simply climbed over the front seat to get to the rear. From 1914 to 1925, all Model Ts were black— Ford said he didn't care what color the customers wanted, so long as it was black.

Think About It?
What differences would it make in your life if the car had never been invented?

Name: _____   Date: _____

Henry Ford and the Assembly Line (cont.)

What Ford did with the assembly-line process was to revolutionize American manufacturing and American life. The auto was no longer the plaything of the rich. By 1950, almost every American family had an auto. Today, many families have two or three. Life was changed. Suburbs grew because people could live farther away from their work.

Moral codes changed and so did American eating and social habits. Highways, superhighways, fast-food restaurants, pollution, and the gasoline shortage became part of the pattern of American life. The assembly line was a good thing—but then, one can also have too much of a good thing.

Graphic Organizer

Directions: Complete the vocabulary chart by creating a definition, using the word in a sentence, and drawing an illustration that helps you remember the meaning of the word.

Word	Definition	Illustration
assembly-line process	Sentence	
Word	Definition	Illustration
duplication	Sentence	

Constructed Response

Why and how did the assembly-line process result in cheaper automobiles? Give specific details or examples to support your answer.

_____

_____

_____

_____

_____

Name: _____   Date: _____

Making Cars on an Assembly Line

Workers at the Highland Park Ford Plant near Detroit, Michigan, in 1908 knew the meaning of the word *dull.* As a bare car chassis moved quickly along a conveyor belt, a worker put the same part or parts on each car. By the time the car rolled off the assembly line, the car was complete. The work required no skill or craftsmanship by the worker. The work was so dull that many workers just quit. Ford stopped some of the people from quitting by offering them five dollars a day. Back then, most people made about fourteen dollars a week, so five dollars a day was a very good wage.

By 1920 using an assembly line, Ford was able to build over a million cars a year. Before he introduced the assembly line, he was only able to build about 18,000 cars a year. Ford did not want to make luxury cars for rich people. Instead, he wanted to make cars that were affordable to the thousands of isolated farmers who lived in the interior of America.

The Model T was introduced in 1908. It was a popular car because it was easy to maintain and repair. It also rode high above the ground, so it could run on bumpy, rutted dirt roads.

Critical Thinking

Ford wanted to make affordable cars for farmers in the nation's interior. Do you think that was a good marketing plan? Give specific details or examples to support your opinion.

_____

_____

_____

_____

Survey

Directions: Survey the students in your classroom about the cars their families own. On your own paper, create a chart with the following headings to record students' responses.

Number of Cars per Family	Make	Model	American Made (Yes or No)

1. What is the average number of cars per family for your class? _____

2. How many students' families own Ford cars or trucks? _____

Name: _____ Date: _____

Industrial Mathematics

Math Calculations

1. In 1870, almost three-fourths of Americans lived on farms or in small farming communities. What fraction of Americans lived in *cities?* _____

2. By 1900, almost one-half of Americans lived in cities. What fraction of Americans lived on farms or in small farming communities? _____

3. In 1875, about 157,000 tons of steel were produced in the United States. By 1910, it was 26 million tons. How many years did it take for this increase in production? _____

4. By 1910, there were 90 buildings in New York and Chicago with more than 10 stories. By 1920, the number had grown to 450. How many more buildings with more than 10 stories were there in 1920 than in 1910? _____

5. In 1870, there were 2,600 telephones in the United States. Three years later, there were an additional 45,400 telephones in the United States. How many telephones were there in 1873? _____

6. The Erie Canal was about 360 miles long. How many kilometers is that? _____

7. A blast furnace today can make about 5,000 tons of iron every day. How many tons of iron can a blast furnace make in seven days? _____

8. In 1882, factories in the United States made 100,000 light bulbs. By 1900, factories made 35 million. How many years did it take to see this increase in production? _____

9. The price of a car dropped from $850 to $360. How much less did someone pay for a car after the price dropped?

   _____

10. At one point before Ford built his assembly line, his company could build 11,000 cars per year. After he introduced the assembly line, his company could make 730,000 cars per year. How many more cars could he make per year with the assembly line than without it?

   _____

Name: _____ Date: _____

Power Statements

True or False

Directions: Read each statement below. Write "T" for true or "F" for false on the line in front of each statement.

_____ 1. Waterwheels and windmills could be used to grind grain.

_____ 2. Waterwheels and windmills always worked.

_____ 3. Steam engines were the first reliable source of power.

_____ 4. Steam-powered factories could be located only in the countryside.

_____ 5. Many people moved to cities where steam-powered factories were located.

_____ 6. Steam-powered factories did not increase production.

_____ 7. Steam-powered factories made more luxuries and goods available to everyone.

_____ 8. Workers had to accept the wages (money) that the factory owner determined.

_____ 9. Steam-powered mills did not produce pollution.

_____ 10. Working conditions became worse for many people.

_____ 11. The pollution from steam-powered factories caused health problems.

_____ 12. Machines replaced craftsmen and women.

_____ 13. Steam locomotives and steamboats made it easier to transport people and goods.

_____ 14. The amount of crime did not increase in large cities.

15. Choose one of the power statements above. If the statement is true, write two or three sentences explaining why it is true. If the statement is false, write two or three sentences explaining why it is false.

_____

_____

_____

_____

_____

UNIT ONE: INDUSTRIALIZATION

Name: _____ Date: _____

Interview an Inventor

Research

Directions: Which inventor fascinated you the most? Samuel Morse? Robert Fulton? Eli Whitney? Henry Ford? Elisha Otis? Orville or Wilbur Wright? Thomas Edison? Michael Faraday? James Watt? Alexander Graham Bell? Choose one of these inventors or select an inventor of your choice.

Imagine that you have the opportunity to interview this inventor. Answer the questions below as that inventor might have done. Use this book, the Internet, or other reference sources if you need help.

Inventor's name: _____

What was your childhood like? _____

_____

_____

_____

How did you get interested in inventing things? _____

_____

_____

_____

Please describe your invention. _____

_____

_____

_____

What was the most frustrating thing that happened as you worked on your invention?

_____

_____

Who helped you in some way? _____

_____

Do you think your invention has changed our country or the world? In what way?

_____

_____

_____

Name: _____ Date: _____

Cool Facts

Cooperative Learning

Directions: Team up with a partner to find the missing word in each cool fact below. Use the Internet and other reference sources if you need help.

1. Guglielmo Marconi invented the "wireless" that used radio waves. When he died in 1937, the world's radio stations were silent for _____ minutes in his honor.

2. The Erie Canal was _____ miles long.

3. Many elevators still use the _____ name, which is the last name of the inventor of the safety elevator.

4. _____ was the first woman doctor of science in Europe. She was also the first woman to receive the Nobel Prize and the first person to receive the Nobel Prize twice.

5. The first food cans had to be opened with a _____ and chisel!

6. Over _____ Model Ts were made in 1922.

7. The first _____ sets had screens that were only about the size of a post-card.

8. Until the 1960s, television pictures were transmitted in _____ only.

9. In 1901, Hubert Booth, a Scotsman, invented an electric machine that sucked in dust. It was so _____ that it had to be pulled from house to house by horses.

10. Henry Ford introduced the Model T in 1908. From 1914 to 1925, the only color it came in was _____ because this color dried more quickly.

11. In 1824, a can of roast veal was taken along on an expedition to the Arctic. The can was opened in _____, a hundred and thirty-four years later. The veal was in perfect condition.

12. A fire in the _____ in 1911 led to legislation requiring improved factory safety standards.

Business Grows in Size and Influence

Thomas Jefferson had dreamed of an America of farmers working for themselves, while Alexander Hamilton's dream was a nation of cities, business, and industry. Until the Civil War, Jefferson's view ruled; but after the war, Hamilton's dream began to develop as the nation's future. A few large manufacturers were better known than some of the of political leaders of the day—everyone knew the names of Rockefeller, Carnegie, Pillsbury, and Armour.

Andrew Carnegie

There were many reasons for the change. Among them were raw materials, new inventions, a cheap labor force, an eager consumer market, government's *laissez faire* (let alone) philosophy, and an enterprising business community willing and able to exploit new opportunities.

America had abundant supplies of most resources needed to become an industrial giant: coal, iron ore, petroleum, and copper, along with agricultural products like corn, wheat, cotton, wool, etc. Technology developed to make these goods into new useful products.

Steel replaced iron with the development of Henry Bessemer's process and the development of the open hearth furnace. Communications improved with a new trans-Atlantic telegraph cable, expansion of the telegraph throughout America, and Alexander Graham Bell's invention of the telephone. Even though many people saw no need for his product, Edwin Drake sank the first oil well in 1859. Within a few years, everyone used kerosene lamps.

Even the food industry was being modernized. Charles Pillsbury found a better way to mill flour. The refrigerator car made meatpacking a major industry and men like Philip Armour and Gustavus Swift prominent.

A large wave of immigration followed the war, and even though many of the newcomers could not speak or write English, they were able to fill unskilled labor jobs. As steamship lines reached more distant ports, immigrants came in larger numbers.

Immigration exceeded 10,000 for the first time from Scandinavia in 1866, Italy in 1880, Russia in 1882, and Poland in 1890. Immigrants not only produced goods, but they were also **consumers**. Many who came remained poor; but at its worst, life in America was usually seen as much better than it had been in their homelands.

With goods being mass-produced, prices dropped, and consumers were always looking for bargains. Department stores first appeared before the Civil War, but they became more common in cities afterward. A & P (Atlantic and Pacific) stores were the first national food chain. In rural areas, people looked forward to receiving their Sears & Roebuck or Montgomery Ward catalogs to buy the same clothes and supplies available in cities.

The United States had no experience with large corporations; so at first, government saw no need to interfere with the way they conducted business. This was called the *laissez faire* policy, from the French phrase meaning "let someone do as they please." The corporations were usually chartered by a state, but most of their money came from other parts of the nation and world. As some corporations got larger, they began to wipe out competitors.

Name: _____ Date: _____

Business Grows in Size and Influence (cont.)

Constructed Response

1. What was the name of the first national food chain? _____

2. What kind of job did immigrants usually fill? _____

3. Which person's dream of the way America should be seemed to come true after the Civil War? _____

Critical Thinking

How could improvements in transportation and communication help other businesses grow? Give specific details or examples to support your opinion.

_____

_____

_____

_____

_____

Graphic Organizer

Directions: Complete the vocabulary chart by creating a definition, using the word in a sentence, and drawing an illustration that helps you remember the meaning of the word.

Word	Definition	Illustration
laissez faire		
	Sentence	
Word	Definition	Illustration
consumers		
	Sentence	

Name: _____   Date: _____

Reflecting on Industrialization

Industrialization provided great benefits for people. Those benefits have made our lives easier and healthier than those of Americans who lived 200 years ago.

Of course, those benefits came at a price. In the past, men, women, and children worked 16 hours or more a day, six days a week. They had to accept the low wages given by factory owners. The factories were not clean, and the machines were often dangerous. Industrialization has also caused pollution of the air and water. Many people today experience a stressful, fast-paced lifestyle because of industrialism.

Critical Thinking

1. List ten benefits of industrialization in your life.

    a. _____

    b. _____

    c. _____

    d. _____

    e. _____

    f. _____

    g. _____

    h. _____

    i. _____

    j. _____

2. Do you think the invention and use of computers represents a new Industrial Revolution? Explain your answer, giving specific details or examples to support your opinion.

    _____

    _____

    _____

    _____

    _____

Captains of Industry or Robber Barons

Lord Acton wrote that "power tends to corrupt, and absolute power corrupts absolutely." In post-Civil War America, power was not in the hands of the man on the street or even elected officials but in the hands of business leaders.

Jay Gould went to Albany with a black bag full of money to bribe the New York legislature. Cornelius Vanderbilt said, "What do I care about the law? Hain't I got the power?" Rich and powerful "captains of industry" (if one admired them) or "robber barons" (if one opposed them) were targets of both great admiration and strong opposition.

Cornelius Vanderbilt

Most of these men started out very poor. Cornelius Vanderbilt's father eked out a living farming and running a small boat between Staten Island and New York City. Jay Gould's father was a poor farmer.

John D. Rockefeller's father was a traveling salesman, and Andrew Carnegie's parents were poor Scottish immigrants who sent him to work in a textile mill for $1.25 a week. Gustavus Swift started in business at the age of 16 with $20 in borrowed money. Eventually, Vanderbilt and Gould became multi-millionaires in railroading, Rockefeller with Standard Oil, Carnegie in steel, and Swift in meatpacking.

As a group, they seemed to enjoy their new wealth *less* than they enjoyed business itself. In many ways, they were very frugal and did not waste money. Vanderbilt decided that painting locomotives in bright colors was too costly, so New York Central painted theirs black.

Philip Armour's meatpacking plants used all of the cow's carcass except hooves. Carnegie controlled every aspect of steelmaking from mining the ore to selling the finished product. Rockefeller watched every step of the oil refining process (down to counting the number of welds on Standard Oil barrels).

John D. Rockefeller

Their goal was to create a monopoly (eliminating all competition). Rockefeller told his salesmen: "Sell *all* the oil in your district." Vanderbilt loved a fight, and he wanted total victory—an opponent beaten into dust and his property wearing the Vanderbilt label. Sometimes these battles were fierce.

Business was a rough game, and at first, there were few rules to control it. Business leaders did many things that would later become illegal. They paid very low wages, disregarded worker safety, bribed judges and legislatures, and bought elections.

Despite their hard-hitting business tactics, many of these businessmen lived by a totally different standard away from work. In their minds, they justified their great wealth in two ways.

One was "social Darwinism," which applied Charles Darwin's theories about "the survival of the fittest" to the business world. Rockefeller compared business to the American Beauty rose: in order to achieve the most beautiful flower at the top, other blooms had to be cut off.

The other philosophy was the "gospel of wealth," which Carnegie supported. It said rich people should use their wealth for the public good. Many good causes were endowed by these very rich Americans.

Name: _____ Date: _____

Captains of Industry or Robber Barons (cont.)

Time Line Activity

Directions: Number the events in order from 1 (first) to 9 (last). Use the time line below for reference.

_____ A.   The Interstate Commerce Act was passed by Congress.

_____ B.   Carnegie retired and devoted his life to philanthropy.

_____ C.   The American Federation of Organized Labor (A.F. of L.) was one of the first federations of labor unions in the United States.

_____ D.   The Standard Oil Company was founded.

_____ E.   The Carnegie Steel Corporation was founded.

_____ F.   Jay Gould attempted to corner the gold market.

_____ G.   Granger Laws passed to regulate grain elevator and railroad freight rates.

_____ H.   The Sherman Anti-Trust Act was passed by Congress. It was the first federal statute to limit cartels and monopolies.

_____ I.   Cornelius Vanderbilt dominated railroads in the east.

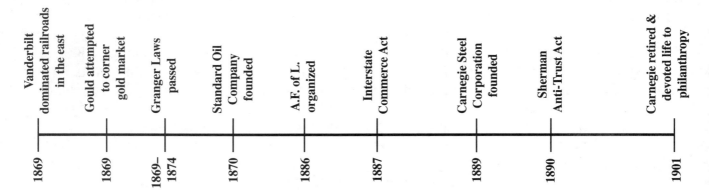

Graphic Organizer

Directions: Complete the chart below by writing the name of the business with which each Captain of Industry was involved.

Captain of Industry	Business
Cornelius Vanderbilt	
Gustavus Swift	
John D. Rockefeller	
Andrew Carnegie	

Name: _____ Date: _____

Industrialization Word Search

Directions: Find and circle the 25 words hidden in the puzzle below. Words may be printed forward, backward, up, down, and diagonally.

```
K Y H S T R A P E L B A E G N A H C R E T N I C
K R E T T N W R C N M H D T N G Z T F Z V Q K R
B G K N Q Z T J C G P D V J N O N W G D M D P N
T N L L T M K A R Y F C R I N Y S T V Q T H X O
G N Y T V I N M Z M X U K Z P T T I R L O F D I
R J D J H A H R P T O C N C L N B V D N E J T T
T T F Q L H C W D M A T T A W Y L Z O E N M T A
T Y G J R M N L R P C Y J T L K L G B K A B E Z
R M F F M N L A T P K R F A P J R Z W H L J X I
R D G H V T M A M A T L E Q U A K X R M P K T L
V N O Z G Q E P P S M E D L P T N Q K T R J I A
N N M I T M Q T P T C X L H L Q O G F E I L L I
M X R P L H T M Z E X K T E V E M M P L A T E R
K D K N M J T P J U K M T A P X F A O W L H S T
M G T V K K W C N R M Z N B L H R E K B P M L S
B C M O N O P O L Y B D K Z L C O F K W I L B U
E I G E N R A C J D E M J M S R C N K C N L W D
Z T P V N H T M N R L X W Y Q H L L E F O B E N
Y R C B H P R Y B K L P K G K X G G B M G R M I
T N R Z R J C I R A S S E M B L Y L I N E N X B
F R Y Z D T L S T E E L M A K I N G H R R P M Y
R P R R R T L Y R K Z D X N D G H T Y G L C C Q
N K B V O J Y W R D T N B R J Z Y H T G K L V K
L V K W F B K B S T E A M E N G I N E N Q L Z P
```

AIRPLANE	EDISON	OIL	TELEPHONE
ARMOUR	FORD	PASTEUR	TEXTILES
ASSEMBLY LINE	INDUSTRIALIZATION	PHONOGRAPH	VANDERBILT
AUTOMOBILE	INTERCHANGEABLE	ROCKEFELLER	WATT
BELL	PARTS	SKYSCRAPER	WHITNEY
CANAL	MEATPACKING	STEAM ENGINE	
CARNEGIE	MONOPOLY	STEELMAKING	

Name: _____ Date: _____

Who Invented It?

Research

Directions: Learn more about the individuals listed in the box. Use the information to answer each question with a name from the box.

Karl Benz	**W. H. Hoover**	**Rudolf Diesel**	**James Watt**
King Camp Gillette	**Henry Ford**	**Clarence Birdseye**	**Samuel Morse**
Alessandro Volta	**Isaac Singer**	**Alexander Graham Bell**	

1. Who invented a lightweight vacuum cleaner in 1908? _____

2. Who invented the safety razor? _____

3. Who invented Morse code? _____

4. The volt, which measures the strength of an electric current, is named after which Italian scientist? _____

5. Who invented modern frozen food? _____

6. Who set up a car company in America? _____

7. A telephone company was named after which inventor?

   _____

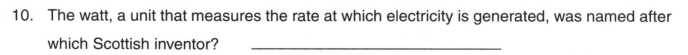

8. Who invented a practical sewing machine?

   _____

9. Who invented the diesel engine?

   _____

10. The watt, a unit that measures the rate at which electricity is generated, was named after which Scottish inventor?   _____

11. Who was the first person to build and run a gasoline-driven car?

    _____

Time Line of the Roaring Twenties: 1920–1929

1913–1921   U.S. President: Woodrow Wilson

1919   The Eighteenth Amendment prohibits the sale of liquor.

1920   U.S. census = 105,710,620 people
The Nineteenth Amendment grants women the right to vote.
The first U.S. cross-country airmail flight is completed.
The average life expectancy in the United States is 54.09 years.

1921–1923   U.S. President: Warren G. Harding

1921   The first skywriting takes place.

1922   *Reader's Digest* magazine is first published.
The first experimental car radios are developed.

1923–1929   U.S. President: Calvin Coolidge

1923   Neon signs are introduced.
A.C. Nielson begins measuring radio audiences.
A speech by President Harding is broadcast on the radio.
Time magazine is first published.
The first Disney cartoon, "Alice's Wonderland," is produced.

1924   The first "perms" for hair are available.
The Teapot Dome Scandal becomes public.
The Model T Ford is sold for $290.

1925   The Goodyear blimp begins sky advertising.
The New Yorker magazine is first published.
The "Grand Ole Opry" radio show begins in Nashville.
Warner Brothers begins experimenting with "talkies" (movies with sound).

1926   The Book-of-the-Month Club begins.
The first radio jingle is broadcast (Wheaties™).
NBC is formed.
Zippers become available.

1927   CBS is formed.
The Holland Tunnel is opened.

1928   The first teletype machine is used.
The first Disney cartoon with sound, "Steamboat Willie," is produced.
The first television sets in the United States are installed in three homes.

1929–1933   U.S. President: Herbert Hoover

1929   The first Academy Awards are presented.
Experiments begin with color television.
The stock market crashes; the Great Depression begins.

Name: _____ Date: _____

The Roaring Twenties Time Line Activity

Directions: Use the time line to answer the following questions.

1. When did zippers become available? _____

2. Who was President of the United States for the majority of the 1920s?

   _____

3. Which amendment in what year granted women the right to vote in the United States?

   _____

4. What was Walt Disney's first cartoon with sound? _____

5. In what year did the stock market crash? _____

6. Name three magazines that were first published in the 1920s.

   _____

7. In how many homes were the first television sets installed in 1928? _____

8. Who was the President of the United States when the decade began?

   _____

9. Who was the President of the United States when the decade ended?

   _____

10. When was the first cross-country airmail flight completed? _____

11. Which product used the first radio jingle? _____

12. When was the Eighteenth Amendment that prohibited the sale of liquor passed? _____

13. What radio show began broadcasting in 1925? _____

14. What flashy advertising item was introduced in 1923? _____

15. When were the first car radios developed? _____

Name: _____   Date: _____

The Decade That Roared

The 1920s was one of the wildest periods in American history. When World War I ended in 1919, Americans looked to the new decade with hope for world peace. The inventions and advancements developed during the war could now be put to peaceful uses. Society rejoiced; people abandoned traditions. New rules were made—and broken.

The Eighteenth Amendment to the Constitution in 1919 made it illegal to import, sell, or manufacture alcoholic beverages—a law that was broken at every level of society.

Rapid advancements in communications, transportation, and technology caused people to coin a new phrase: "What will they think of next?"

Electricity was so new that many people were afraid of it. They bought special caps to put over electrical outlets so the electricity wouldn't spill out into the room. In 1919, only about one-third of American homes had electricity. That number had doubled by 1929.

With the introduction of the assembly line, car manufacturers began producing great numbers of automobiles at a much lower cost. In 1924, people could buy a brand new Ford Model T for $290. Over 23,000,000 cars jammed American roads by 1929.

At the beginning of the decade, movies were black and white and had no sound. Warner Brothers introduced the first color film, complete with sound, in 1929.

Passage of the Nineteenth Amendment granting women the right to vote ushered in a new era of freedom for women, who began wearing new hairstyles and daring dresses so short, they showed their knees in public!

People were anxious to put thoughts of war behind them and enjoy life with a vigor never seen before. Although the decade began on a high note, it ended with fear of economic ruin. The good times came to an end with the Stock Market Crash of 1929.

Critical Thinking

1. List ten items in your home that wouldn't work without electricity.

   _____

   _____

   _____

2. Of those items, which would you miss most? Why? Give specific details or examples to support your opinion.

   _____

   _____

   _____

   _____

Name: _____ Date: _____

Prohibition Becomes the Law

For decades many **temperance** groups, led mainly by women and various religious organizations, had tried to make alcohol illegal in the United States. Some blamed alcohol for the rising rate in divorces, family problems, crimes, violence, and poverty. Others felt the grain used to make alcohol could be better used for food.

By 1916, 23 of the 48 states had passed anti-saloon laws that closed taverns and prohibited the manufacture of intoxicating beverages. In 1919, the Eighteenth Amendment to the U.S. Constitution made the manufacture, sale, import, or export of liquor illegal anywhere in the United States.

The Eighteenth Amendment did not make it illegal to possess liquor or to drink it. Exceptions were also made for liquor sold for medicinal, sacramental, and industrial purposes. It also excluded fruit and grape beverages prepared for personal use at home.

Congress passed the Volstead Act to enforce Prohibition, but the government had too little money and too few people to be effective.

Even though all taverns and saloons were officially closed, illegal taverns and nightclubs—called **speakeasies**—sprang up everywhere. People smuggled liquor across the border from Canada, imported it illegally from Europe and the Caribbean Islands, and produced it in illegal factories. Prohibition gave criminals a wonderful opportunity to grow rich by providing **bootleg** alcohol.

Matching

_____ 1. temperance
_____ 2. bootleg
_____ 3. speakeasies

a. illegal taverns or nightclubs
b. moderate or no use of alcoholic beverages
c. alcohol produced and/or imported illegally

Critical Thinking

Do you think the government has the right to ban alcohol, tobacco, drugs, or any other product? Why or why not? Use specific details or examples to support your opinion.

_____

_____

_____

_____

_____

Name: _____ Date: _____

Warren G. Harding

Born: November 2, 1865
Term of office: March 4, 1921–
        August 2, 1923
Occupation: Newspaper publisher
Political Party: Republican

When World War I finally ended, Warren Harding believed the country needed a "return to normalcy," and that became his campaign slogan.

Harding stressed Americanism and offered hope to people tired of war. He arranged a peace treaty signed with Germany in 1921. With Charles G. Dawes as director, the national budget was cut from six billion to three billion dollars, and at the end of 1922, there was even a surplus.

Rumors of scandal, corruption, and dishonest deals at high levels in the government began in 1922. Although Harding himself was not accused of wrongdoing, his administration is remembered for its corruption.

Charles R. Forbes, head of the Veterans Bureau and a personal friend of Harding's, was tried for bribery and conspiracy. He had authorized hundreds of millions of dollars for overpriced materials, sites, and construction.

Warren G. Harding

Secretary of the Interior Albert Fall was convicted of accepting an illegal payment of $400,000 in return for turning over two valuable tracts of land to private oil companies.

Attorney General Harry Daughtery, another close friend of Harding's, stood trial twice for conspiring to defraud the government by selling government favors. Both times, the juries were not able to determine a verdict, and the case was finally dropped.

UNIT TWO: THE ROARING TWENTIES

Constructed Response

Warren G. Harding's administration is known for corruption. Give three examples of corruption in his administration. Be sure to give specific details or examples to support your answer.

_____

_____

_____

_____

_____

_____

_____

_____

_____

_____

Name: _____ Date: _____

Women Finally Allowed to Vote

Nineteenth Amendment

The right of citizens of the United States to vote shall not be denied or abridged by the United States or any state on account of sex.

The campaign for women's suffrage (the right to vote) began in the 1840s, long before the Nineteenth Amendment was finally ratified in 1920. Many states had granted women full or partial suffrage before 1920. The election of 1920 was the first time all women were allowed to vote for the president.

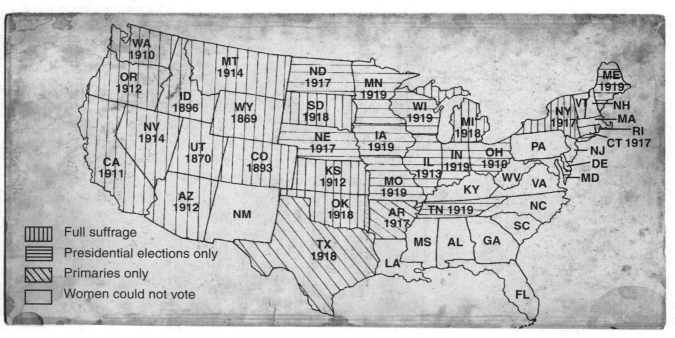

Map Skills

1. List five states that did not allow women the right to vote before the Nineteenth Amendment was passed.

   _____

2. List five states that allowed women to vote in all elections before the Nineteenth Amendment was passed.

   _____

3. Geographically, what stands out about states that had granted women the right to vote before the Nineteenth Amendment was passed and those that hadn't? Give specific details or examples to support your answer.

   _____

   _____

Name: _____ Date: _____

Flaming Youth

A social revolution took place among young people during the twenties. Nicknamed the "Flaming Youth," they lived for pleasure, enjoyed fast-paced music and vigorous dances, wore "scandalous" fashions and hairdos, and developed a taste for zany stunts like flagpole sitting and marathon dances.

Young women called "flappers" began dressing in ways that outraged their parents. Previously, women's dresses had covered them completely from neck to ankles. Suddenly, fashions changed. Necklines plunged, and hemlines rose above the knees.

Young women defied authority by wearing make-up, smoking cigarettes, and cutting their hair short.

In Utah, lawmakers tried to make it illegal for women to wear "skirts higher than three inches above the ankle."

Marathons became the craze in the twenties. Dance marathons went on nonstop for days. The last couple standing won a prize. Other marathon events included kissing contests, roller-skating, and flagpole sitting.

Did You Know?

Gertrude Ederle, age 19, became the first American woman to swim the English Channel on August 26, 1926. She did it in a record-breaking time of 14 hours and 31 minutes.

Constructed Response

Why were young people of the twenties nicknamed the "Flaming Youth?" Give specific details or examples to support your answer.

_____

_____

_____

Graphic Organizer

Directions: Every generation has fashions in clothing, jewelry, or hairstyles that defy parental authority. On the T-Chart below, list the fashions in clothing, jewelry, or hairstyles that pertain to the twenties and today.

Flappers of the Twenties	Teenagers of Today

Name: _____ Date: _____

Americans on the Go

Henry Ford built his first car in 1896. By 1908, the Ford Motor Company had produced a simple, reliable car called the Model T. Nicknamed the Tin Lizzie, its 20-horsepower engine allowed drivers to reach a top speed of 40 miles per hour. Henry Ford announced, "a customer could have the car in any color as long as it was black." This was true from 1914 to 1925.

Model T

Early Fords cost $850—a very high price for the times. At first, cars were considered "toys" only the very rich could afford. That changed when Ford introduced an efficient assembly line for production. The price of a new Ford dropped to $290 in 1924.

The Ford Motor Company described the Model T as "an inexpensive vehicle for the great multitude." People could buy cars on the installment plan.

In 1927, the Ford Motor Company discontinued making the Model T and replaced it with the more modern Model A, which sold for $395.

Even at under $300 dollars, owning a car usually meant either saving for a long time or buying on credit. Most women did not have jobs outside the home. Men working at good jobs in the auto industry made between $5 and $7 per day and worked six-day weeks during the twenties. Most jobs paid much less.

Model A

True or False

Directions: Circle "T" for True or "F" for False.

1. T   F   Henry Ford built his first car in 1897.
2. T   F   The nickname of the Model T was the "Tin Lizzie."
3. T   F   The top speed of a Model T was 40 miles an hour.
4. T   F   The early Fords cost approximately $2,000.
5. T   F   Using the assembly line for production caused the price of a new Ford to drop.
6. T   F   People could not buy cars on an installment plan.
7. T   F   The Model T was replaced by the Model A.
8. T   F   For most of its production run, the Model T was available only in the color black.
9. T   F   Most women did not have jobs outside the home.
10. T   F   Men employed in the auto industry worked six-day weeks.

Name: _____ Date: _____

Automobiles Change America

Mass production of automobiles affected both society and the economy. As more people bought cars, more jobs were created in the auto industry, and wages rose. The demand for cars also created more jobs in industries that made steel, glass, rubber, petroleum, and other products used to build cars.

In a widely reported interview of the time, a farm wife was asked why her family owned a car but not a bathtub. "You can't go to town in a bathtub," she replied.

As more people drove cars, the roads became very crowded. People demanded a better road system and better roads. In 1909, the United States had only 750 miles of paved roads. By 1930, that number had risen to more than 100,000 miles.

Road construction provided jobs for crews and suppliers of materials. As more roads were built, people traveled more. Along the new roads, businesses like gas stations, diners, hot-dog stands, and tourist cabins grew to meet the demand of travelers.

Car dealers and used car lots were seen for the first time. The first modern gas stations opened in 1913. By 1929, the country had 121,500—an average of more than one per mile of paved road!

Not only did automobile companies make cars, they also built millions of taxis, buses, and trucks. Between 1904 and 1929, the number of trucks registered in the United States rose from 700 to 3.4 million.

Did You Know?
The first U.S. federal tax on gasoline was enacted in 1932. The rate back then? A penny per gallon.

UNIT TWO: THE ROARING TWENTIES

Political Cartoon

Directions: Draw a political cartoon about what the farm wife above might have said about any other aspect of owning a car in the 1920s.

Name: _____ Date: _____

Welcome to the Jazz Age

Jazz is a uniquely American style of music that evolved from spirituals, blues, and ragtime. Jazz first burst forth in the early 1900s in New Orleans. At first jazz featured enthusiasm, volume, and improvisation rather than finesse. Early jazz was performed mainly by small marching bands or solo pianists and became popular at weddings, picnics, parades, and funerals.

Although jazz developed among black musicians, no sound recordings remain of the earliest jazz groups. The first jazz recording in 1917 was by an all-white group who called themselves the Original Dixieland Jazz Band. Eventually New Orleans-style jazz as played by whites came to be called **Dixieland jazz**.

Jazz in the 1920s involved great experimentation and discovery. For the first time, bands began featuring soloists on trumpet, saxophone, and piano. Mamie Smith had a sudden hit in 1920 with her recording of "Crazy Blues." One of the greatest jazz singers of the twenties was Bessie Smith.

Many New Orleans jazz musicians, including Louis Armstrong and Jelly Roll Morton, became famous by performing in Chicago nightclubs. Eventually a Chicago style of jazz evolved, derived from the New Orleans style, but with more emphasis on soloists and often featuring saxophones, pianos, and vocalists. **Chicago jazz** had tenser rhythms and more complicated textures. Throughout the 1920s and into the 1930s, jazz continued to be a very popular form of music.

Constructed Response

What is the difference between Dixieland jazz and Chicago jazz? Give specific details or examples to support your answer. You may want to listen to examples of each type of jazz music.

_____

_____

_____

_____

_____

_____

_____

_____

_____

_____

Name: _____ Date: _____

Louis Armstrong

Born about 1901 in New Orleans, Louis Armstrong spent his first 12 years in a very poor home. His father had deserted the family. They seldom had enough to eat or decent clothing, and Louis dropped out of school after fifth grade.

When he was about 13, Louis was sent to the Colored Waifs' Home where he joined a boys' brass band. With Louis' natural ability for music as a cornet player, he soon became the star of the group. After he left the home, he played in rough clubs and dance halls in the urban slum districts of New Orleans. He couldn't afford his own cornet and had to borrow one to perform.

Louis became friends with King Oliver, a famous black musician. After becoming part of Kid Orvy's band, his reputation grew. In 1922, Louis joined Oliver's Creole Jazz Band in Chicago.

Two years later, he joined a band in New York where he dazzled both musicians and audiences with his unique loose, springy swing style and his ability to improvise.

Previously, most jazz was played by ensembles. Rarely was any one person featured for other than a short solo. Back in Chicago in 1925, Louis led his own band and began making records playing New Orleans style

Raised in poverty, Louis Armstrong became famous as a jazz trumpet player and singer. By the 1950s, Louis Armstrong had performed all over the world and was the most famous jazz musician of the time.

jazz. The popularity of his short solos soon convinced record companies that he should be featured with other players merely providing backup.

At first, his records featured Louis playing the trumpet. Then he began singing in a rough voice that attracted listeners. His hit songs included "Savoy Blues," "Hotter Than That," "West End Blues," "Blueberry Hill," "Mack the Knife," "Hello, Dolly," and "What a Wonderful World."

Technology in the Classroom

Directions: Use an Internet search engine to locate the answer to the following question.

One of Louis Armstrong's songs hit number one on the charts in 1964. What was the name of the song?

_____

Name: _____   Date: _____

John Calvin Coolidge

As governor of Massachusetts, Calvin Coolidge attracted national attention when he called out the National Guard in response to a strike of the Boston police.

"There is no right to strike against the public safety by anybody, anywhere, anytime," he said.

Coolidge was elected vice president under President Harding in 1920. When the president died on August 2, 1923, Coolidge became president. His first challenge was to clean up the corruption that had occurred while Harding was president.

Farmers in the western part of the country did not enjoy the prosperity of the twenties. They wanted government aid, but Coolidge refused. Congress approved the McNary-Haugen Farm Relief Bill, which proposed that the government buy surplus crops and sell them abroad to raise domestic agricultural prices.

Coolidge vetoed the bill in 1927 and again in 1928 because he felt the government had no business fixing prices.

Throughout his term as president, Coolidge retained very conservative policies. He opposed government intervention in private business.

John Calvin Coolidge decided not to run for another term as president in 1928. When asked why, he replied, "Because there's no chance for advancement."

Critical Thinking

Coolidge believed that the government should not interfere with private business. Do you agree or disagree? Why? Give specific details or examples to support your answer.

_____

_____

_____

_____

_____

Research

Directions: Use reference sources to answer these questions about President Coolidge.

1. When and where was he born? _____

2. What was his nickname? _____

3. What political party did he belong to? _____

4. What was his occupation before going into politics? _____

5. What was his campaign slogan in the 1924 presidential election? _____

_____

Name: _____   Date: _____

What Could You Buy for a Dollar?

During the twenties, a dollar went a long way. However, most kids only received about ten cents a week for allowance, so it took a long time to save a dollar.

Graphic Organizer

Directions: Compare the cost of an item in the twenties to the price of a similar item today.

Item	Twenties	Today
Movie ticket		
Gallon of milk		
Pack of gum		
Candy bar		
Ice cream bar		

Name: _____   Date: _____

Learning a New Language: Jive Talk

Many slang words and phrases came into common use in the 1920s. If you thought someone was handing you a line of nonsense, you might tell them to "stop the banana oil." You could compliment a woman by telling her she was "the eel's ankles," "the bee's knees," or "the cat's meow." A stylish young man might be called a "sheik." But beware if someone says you're a "flat tire," because they think you're a boring person.

Matching

Directions: Match these twenties terms with their definitions. Feel free to use a dictionary, the Internet, or other resources to find the answers.

_____ 1. speakeasy	a.	woman's short haircut
_____ 2. bootleg	b.	an illegal tavern or nightclub
_____ 3. guff	c.	dressed up; looking good
_____ 4. half-pint	d.	posh; elegant
_____ 5. hep	e.	being lazy
_____ 6. flapper	f.	a child
_____ 7. bob	g.	tease
_____ 8. razz	h.	back talk
_____ 9. smackeroo	i.	wool pajamas with feet
_____ 10. spiffy	j.	just great
_____ 11. two bits	k.	feet
_____ 12. horsefeathers	l.	with it; up-to-date
_____ 13. lollygagging	m.	illegal
_____ 14. mob	n.	a dollar
_____ 15. ritzy	o.	a quarter
_____ 16. dogs	p.	gangsters
_____ 17. Dr. Dentons	q.	nonsense
_____ 18. the berries	r.	stylish young woman

Name: _____   Date: _____

Twenties Internet Scavenger Hunt

Technology in the Classroom

Directions: To complete this scavenger hunt, use the Internet to locate the answers to these questions.

J.E. Clair, owner of the Acme Packing Company, bought a pro football franchise on August 27, 1921. He named the team in honor of the workers at his meat processing plant.

1. What did he name the team? _____

The National Football League franchise in Decatur, Illinois, was transferred to another city in Illinois in January 1922.

2. What team did they become? _____

In April 1923, the Firestone Tire and Rubber Company of Akron, Ohio, began the first regular production of a new product.

3. What was the product? _____

Rin Tin Tin became a famous movie star in 1923.

4. What was Rin Tin Tin? _____

The first African-American basketball team was organized in 1927.

5. What was the name of the team? _____

The first Miss America pageant was held in 1921.

6. Who was the winner? _____

The first woman to become a state governor took office in Wyoming on January 5, 1925.

7. What was her name? _____

Charles Lindbergh took off from Roosevelt Field in New York on May 20, 1927, in a small airplane. He flew nonstop to Paris, France.

8. What was the name of his plane? _____

9. How long did the flight last? _____

Penicillin was discovered in 1928.

10. Who discovered it? _____

UNIT TWO: THE ROARING TWENTIES

Name: _____   Date: _____

Up, Up, and Away

In 1903, the Wright brothers successfully flew an airplane for the first time. They didn't fly very far, very high, or for very long—but they did fly.

Early planes were not too reliable and were considered more of a curiosity than a future means of transportation. During World War I, however, development of airplanes progressed dramatically as military leaders realized their value both for **surveillance** and as weapons.

By the mid twenties, planes had become more dependable and capable of longer flights. People began to realize their potential as a new form of transportation for both people and **cargo**.

In 1927, Charles Lindbergh set a cross-country record when he flew from San Diego, California, to New York in 21 hours and 20 minutes. (He stopped overnight at St. Louis, Missouri.) Ten days later, Lindbergh made his most famous flight when he became the first pilot to fly solo across the Atlantic Ocean from New York to Paris, France.

Did You Know?
"Elm Farm Ollie" became the first cow to fly in an airplane in 1930. While in flight over St. Louis, the cow was milked. The milk was sealed in little paper containers and then parachuted over the city.

Graphic Organizer

Directions: Complete the vocabulary chart by creating a definition, using the word in a sentence, and drawing an illustration that helps you remember the meaning of the word.

Word	Definition	Illustration
surveillance		
	Sentence	
Word	Definition	Illustration
cargo		
	Sentence	

UNIT TWO: THE ROARING TWENTIES

Name: _____   Date: _____

Who's Who?

Matching

Directions: Many Americans became famous in the twenties and thirties. Use reference sources if you need help matching these people with their areas of fame.

Actress/Actor	**Anthropologist**	**Artist**	**Author**	**Baseball player**
Boxer	**Composer**	**Dancer**	**Film maker**	**Football player**
Golfer	**Magician**	**Musician**	**Olympic medal winner**	
Pilot	**Singer**	**Tennis player**		

1. _____ Marian Anderson

2. _____ Jelly Roll Morton

3. _____ Fred Astaire

4. _____ Pearl S. Buck

5. _____ Charlie Chaplin

6. _____ Douglas Corrigan

7. _____ Jack Dempsey

8. _____ Walt Disney

9. _____ Amelia Earhart

10. _____ George Gershwin

11. _____ Benny Goodman

12. _____ Red Grange

13. _____ Jean Harlow

14. _____ Harry Houdini

15. _____ Bobby Jones

16. _____ Joe Louis

17. _____ Margaret Mead

18. _____ Duke Ellington

19. _____ Jesse Owens

20. _____ Babe Ruth

21. _____ Bessie Smith

22. _____ John Steinbeck

23. _____ Big Bill Tilden

24. _____ Gene Tunney

25. _____ Johnny Weissmuller

Amelia Earhart

Babe Ruth

UNIT TWO: THE ROARING TWENTIES

Name: _____   Date: _____

The Other Side of the Coin

Not everyone in the twenties had a decade of good times. When people today read about Prohibition, gangsters, speakeasies, bootleg liquor, flappers, jive talk, dance marathons, and jazz, it's easy to get the impression gangsters hung around every street corner and all Americans partied every night.

Although the decade was marked by fun and extravaganza, not everyone lived that way. In fact, the majority of people, especially middle- and lower-class families, probably lived much the way you do now. Children went to school. They did chores around the house. They spent time with friends and family.

For some groups like African Americans, farmers, and newly arrived immigrants, the twenties didn't roar at all. Economic conditions had changed little for African Americans in the south since the time of slavery. Prejudice was still strong. Schools and public buildings remained segregated. Farmers in the twenties did what farmers have done for thousands of years. They plowed their fields, planted their crops, and prayed for good weather and a good harvest. Immigrants also met prejudice as they tried to learn a new language, find jobs, and become part of a new country.

Graphic Organizer

Directions: Fill in the chart to show similarities and differences between children in the 1920s and children today.

	1920s only	Now only	Then & Now
Attend school			
Watch movies			
Play video games			
Play baseball			
Help around the house			
Play board games like checkers			
Watch TV			
Listen to the radio			
Play with dolls			
Roller skate			
Ride skateboards			
Build snowmen			
Read books			

Name: _____   Date: _____

Evolution on Trial

In 1925, high school biology teacher John T. Scopes was accused of violating the Butler Act. This Tennessee law made it illegal for a teacher in any state-supported public school or college to teach any theory of evolution because it contradicted the Bible's account of man's creation.

Tennessee's Governor Austin Peay said, "The very integrity of the Bible in its statement of man's divine creation is denied by any theory that man descended or has ascended from any lower order of animals."

Opponents to the law believed it was a violation of the Constitution, which insures the separation of church and state.

The trial of John Scopes gained worldwide media attention. Members of the press referred to it as the "Monkey Trial" because many people thought that evolution meant humans had descended from monkeys.

John T. Scopes

The defense attorney, Clarence Darrow, argued that evolution was a valid scientific theory. He also attempted to convince the jury that the Butler Act was unconstitutional. However, he did not deny that Scopes had broken the law. Scopes was convicted and fined $100.

Darrow stated that this was "the first case of its kind since we stopped trying people for witchcraft."

The verdict was later reversed by the state supreme court, but the Butler Act remained on the books in Tennessee until 1967.

Critical Thinking

Clarence Darrow's defense was that the law was wrong. If a law is wrong, do you think that makes it all right to ignore or break it? Give specific details or examples to support your opinion.

_____

_____

_____

_____

_____

_____

_____

_____

_____

UNIT TWO: THE ROARING TWENTIES

Name: _____ Date: _____

Review the Twenties

Matching

Directions: Match the definition in the right column with the corresponding term in the left column. Use the Internet or reference sources if you need help.

_____ 1. Charlie Chaplin	a. A group of musicians
_____ 2. suffrage	b. Baseball player
_____ 3. ensemble	c. A comedian who starred in movies
_____ 4. The Noble Experiment	d. A type of automobile
_____ 5. improvise	e. Dressed up
_____ 6. Model A	f. Another term for Prohibition
_____ 7. Dixieland	g. Make up as you go along
_____ 8. Gertrude Ederle	h. Right to vote
_____ 9. spiffy	i. Swam the English Channel
_____ 10. Babe Ruth	j. A style of jazz

True or False

Directions: Circle "T" for True or "F" for False.

1. T F The 1920s were nicknamed the Roaring Twenties because people played their radios so loud all of the time.

2. T F During the twenties, cars had a major influence on Americans.

3. T F Calvin Coolidge's administration was marked by scandal and corruption.

4. T F Charles Lindbergh made the first solo flight across the Atlantic Ocean.

5. T F Women who cut their hair short and wore short skirts and makeup were called flappers.

6. T F Although jazz began in the twenties, it didn't become popular until the sixties.

7. T F Warren G. Harding died while president.

8. T F Jazz combined rock and roll, opera, and classical music into a new form.

9. T F Louis Armstrong grew up in a rich home in New York City.

10. T F None of the movies made during the twenties or thirties were Westerns.

Time Line of the Great Depression: 1929–1939

1929–1933   U.S. President: Herbert Hoover
1930   U.S. census = 122,775,046 people
            "Blondie and Dagwood" becomes a daily comic strip.
            The National Unemployed Council is formed.
1931   Commercial teletype service begins.
            "The Star-Spangled Banner" becomes the national anthem.
            The Empire State Building is opened.
            The Davis-Bacon Act provides for the payment of prevailing wages to workers
                employed on public works projects.
1932   The Lindbergh baby is kidnapped.
            The first Winter Olympics held in the United States are held at Lake Placid, NY.
            Unemployment reaches 13,000,000.
            The Norris-LaGuardia Act prohibits federal injunctions in labor disputes.
            The cost of mailing a letter rises from two cents to three cents.
1933–1945   U.S. President: Franklin D. Roosevelt
1933   Franklin D. Roosevelt begins radio "Fireside Chats."
            The first real comic book is published: *Funnies on Parade.*
            The Twenty-First Amendment repeals Prohibition.
            The National Industrial Recovery Act guarantees the rights of employees to or-
                ganize and bargain collectively.
            Frances Perkins becomes Secretary of Labor (first woman named to a presidential
                Cabinet).
            The first drive-in movie theater opens (Camden, NJ).
            Minimum wage is set at 40 cents an hour.
1934   "High-fidelity" records become available.
            One-half of the homes in the United States have radios.
1935   IBM begins selling electric typewriters.
            The Social Security Act is signed.
1936   The BBC begins the world's first television service, three hours a day.
            The electric guitar is invented.
            LIFE, the magazine, is first published.
1937   The electrical digital calculator is invented.
            A child labor law is passed.
            Nylon is invented.
            Look magazine is first published.
            The Golden Gate Bridge opens.
1938   Disney produces its first full-length animated film, *Snow White and the Seven
                Dwarfs.*
            The Fair Labor Standards Act establishes the 40-hour work week, the minimum
                wage, and bans child labor in interstate commerce.
            Superman was "born."
1939   Television is demonstrated at the New York World's Fair.
            World War II begins in Europe.

UNIT THREE: THE GREAT DEPRESSION

Name: _____ Date: _____

The Great Depression Time Line Activity

Directions: Use the time line to answer the following questions.

1. When and where were the first Winter Olympics in the United States held?

   _____

2. What were two magazines first published in the 1930s?

   _____

3. What was the title of Disney's first full-length animated movie?

   _____

4. Who was the President of the United States in 1937? _____

5. When did "The Star-Spangled Banner" become the official national anthem? _____

6. How many homes in the United States had radios in 1934? _____

7. Which opened first, the Golden Gate Bridge or the Empire State Building?

   _____

8. How much did it cost to mail a letter in 1932? _____

9. Who was the first woman to became a member of the president's Cabinet?

   _____

10. How many people were unemployed in 1932? _____

11. What was minimum wage in 1933? _____

12. Which amendment repealed Prohibition? _____

13. When was the Social Security Act signed? _____

14. Which were available first: electric guitars, electric typewriters, or electric calculators?

    _____

15. What was the name of the first comic book published? _____

Name: _____ Date: _____

The Millionaire Miner

When Herbert Hoover graduated with a mining engineering degree in 1895, he had $40 in his pocket and no job prospects. He ended up working for $2.50 a day as a pick-and-shovel miner in a California gold mine. With his experience, hard work, talents, and ambition, Hoover quickly rose above hard physical labor.

At age 23, he managed a successful gold mine in Western Australia. From there, he went to China as a mining consultant. He spent time with other mining operations in Europe, Russia, Southwest Asia, and Africa.

By 1908, Hoover owned a worldwide business with offices in France, England, and the United States and was a millionaire several times over.

Although he probably could have made another fortune during World War I when the demand for ore and metal increased greatly, Hoover agreed to head the Commission for Relief in Belgium. He worked without pay to organize a successful relief program to feed ten million starving people in Belgium. Then he accepted the position of Food Administrator

Before becoming president, Hoover led a colorful life. Orphaned at the age of eight, he was raised by his uncle in Oregon. While at Stanford University, Hoover founded his own fraternity: the Barbarians.

in the United States and later, Chief of the Supreme Allied Economic Council.

Hoover's success led to his appointment as Secretary of Commerce under Presidents Harding and Coolidge. When Coolidge chose not to seek reelection in 1928, the Republicans nominated Hoover.

UNIT THREE: THE GREAT DEPRESSION

Critical Thinking

From what you read, what impresses you the most about Herbert Hoover? Give specific details or examples to support your answer.

_____

_____

_____

_____

_____

_____

_____

Name: _____ Date: _____

The Crash Heard Around the World

Throughout the twenties, people spent money much more freely than ever before. More products were available; more people had jobs, and wages were higher. People bought on credit. As stock prices steadily climbed throughout the decade, people often invested everything they had, mortgaged their homes, and even borrowed money to buy stocks. They thought the prosperity of the twenties would last forever.

In the fall of 1929, investors who had bought stocks on credit began to sell. As more stocks sold, prices fell. Investors panicked, especially those who had bought stocks on margin (bought at a lower price, promising to pay the rest later). Between Black Thursday (October 24, 1929) and Terrible Tuesday (October 29, 1929) so many shares of stock were sold that the market collapsed completely. In one day, stock values dropped $10–$15 billion.

Not all Americans had invested in the stock market, but almost everyone felt an immediate effect of the crash. Most Americans kept their savings in banks that had invested the funds in the stock market. When the stock market crashed, the banks couldn't return the money to investors. In one terrible week, rich, middle-class, and poor people lost everything.

Over 1,300 banks went broke in 1930. Another 2,300 failed the following year. The stock market crash brought the good times of the twenties to a screeching halt. Although no one yet realized the extent of the problem, the stock market crash began the Great Depression, which lasted until the mid 1940s.

Unemployment went from three percent in 1925 to 25 percent in 1932. Many people who still had jobs were required to take cuts in pay to keep their jobs.

Graphic Organizer

Directions: Fill in the flowchart to illustrate the paragraph below.

As more people lost their jobs, they had less money to spend. Less people spending money meant stores sold fewer products and needed fewer workers. Since fewer products were purchased, factories produced less, and more people lost their jobs.

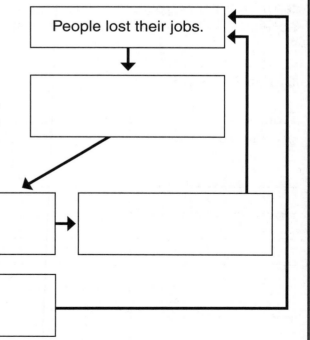

People lost their jobs.

Name: _____ Date: _____

The 1930s

The 1920s may have begun with a bang, but the 1930s opened with a crash. The effects of the October 1929 Stock Market Crash echoed across the nation as the new decade began. Investors lost tens of billions of dollars. Over a million people lost their life savings in the stock market crash. Even those who had no money in stocks felt the chain reaction that resulted.

People in the thirties faced many new challenges as businesses and industries shut down and banks collapsed. Millions of people found themselves unemployed and homeless. Schools closed in rural areas. An estimated 2.2 million children were not attending school in 1933. Between 1930 and 1935, as many as 750,000 farms were lost because of bankruptcy.

President Herbert Hoover underestimated the severity of the problem as he assured people that the crisis was "a passing incident in our national lives." Hoover did not believe the federal government should pro-vide relief or jobs to individuals. He thought private charities, together with city and state governments, were responsible for helping those in need.

During the thirties, many people relied on soup kitchens for food. They stood in bread lines to buy day-old bread. They looked to the government to solve the massive unemployment problem. Men walked around with their pockets turned inside out to show they were broke. Millions learned to make do with what they had, because they couldn't afford new clothing, furniture, appliances, or automobiles.

Advances in technology, communications, and transportation continued but at a much slower pace than in the previous decade.

Think About It
What if you had been a child during the Great Depression? What could you have done to help your family get through?

Critical Thinking

Do you agree or disagree with Hoover that charities instead of the government were responsible for those in need? Why? Give specific details or examples to support your opinion.

_____

_____

_____

_____

_____

_____

Name: _____   Date: _____

What's New?

Directions: Circle all the products that were introduced in the twenties and thirties and that people still use today.

1920   Pogo™ sticks

1921   Band-Aids™
          Wrigley's™ gum

1922   Eskimo Pie™
          The Reader's Digest magazine

1923   Welch's™ grape jelly
          Time magazine

1924   Wheaties™ cereal
          spiral-bound notebooks
          Kleenex™
          crossword puzzle books
          permanents for hair

1925   *The New Yorker* magazine

1926   zippers

1927   Hostess™
          cakes

1928   Rice Krispies™

1930   Nancy Drew mysteries

1931   Scotch™ Tape
          electric razors
          Scrabble™
          Alka-Seltzer™

1933   Mickey Mouse™ watches
          comic books

1934   hi-fi records

1935   paperback books
          electric typewriters
          MONOPOLY™ game first sold by
             Parker Brothers
          parking meters

1936   electric guitars
          Life magazine

1937   nylon
          Look magazine
          Wheat Chex™

1938   *Jack and Jill*
          magazine

1939   air-conditioned cars

Do you use any of the above products? Which ones?

_____

_____

_____

_____

Name: _____ Date: _____

Herbert Hoover, President

Born: August 10, 1874
Term as President: March 4, 1929, to
    March 4, 1933
Political Party: Republican

President Herbert Hoover

During Hoover's presidential campaign, the country was flourishing. Most people expected the economic prosperity to continue indefinitely. In a spirit of optimism, Hoover promised "… a chicken in every pot and a car in every garage."

Although the economic prosperity of the twenties continued in most industries until the stock market crash, farmers were already having problems. As they increased efficiency and put more land into farming, prices dropped. Trying to produce more crops made prices drop even lower.

In response, Congress passed the Agricultural Marketing Act of 1929, which established the first large-scale aid to farmers during peacetime.

Although Hoover began his term as president on an optimistic note, that ended less than eight months later when the stock market crashed in October 1929, plunging the United States into what became known as the Great Depression.

After the Depression began, farm prices continued to drop. By 1932, government funds ran out, and prices plunged to a new low.

Hoover went from being a very popular president to one of the most disliked men in America. By the 1932 presidential election, the entire country had been affected. Hoover did not have a chance for reelection.

Did You Know?

After World War II ended, Europe was suffering from a famine caused by war. President Harry Truman asked former President Hoover to help with this situation. Hoover became the honorary chairman of the Famine Emergency Committee. He traveled around the world asking countries to donate food for Europe.

Critical Thinking

Hoover promised "…a chicken in every pot and a car in every garage." What do you think he really meant by that? Give specific details or examples to support your answer.

_____

_____

_____

_____

_____

_____

UNIT THREE: THE GREAT DEPRESSION

Franklin D. Roosevelt

Born: January 30, 1882, in Hyde Park,
New York
Profession: Lawyer
Term as President: March 4, 1933, to
April 12, 1945
Political Party: Democratic

Franklin D. Roosevelt grew up in a wealthy New York family. Theodore Roosevelt was his fifth cousin. He spent summers vacationing in Europe and never attended school until he was 14 years old. His family provided private **tutors**, and his mother supervised his education.

As a young man, Roosevelt enjoyed bird watching and **natural history**. He enjoyed sports, particularly swimming and hiking. Reading adventure stories and stamp collecting were two of his other favorite pastimes.

In 1896, Roosevelt attended Groton School, a private preparatory school in Massachusetts. He went on to Harvard and then to Columbia Law School in 1904. Against his mother's advice, he married **Eleanor Roosevelt**, a distant cousin who was Theodore Roosevelt's niece.

Roosevelt's early political career included two terms in the New York state senate (1910–1913) and an appointment as assistant secretary of the Navy (1913–1920). He resigned to campaign for the vice presidency in 1920 but lost the election.

As a result of the disease **polio**, Roosevelt lost the use of his legs in 1921. He was unable to walk without crutches. His mother wanted him to retire from politics, but Roosevelt had other ideas.

**Franklin D. Roosevelt,
Assistant Secretary of the Navy
1913**

With the help of his wife, Roosevelt remained active behind the scenes until he ran for governor of New York in 1928. Most people were unaware of the extent of his disability when he was governor and later president.

In 1928, the Republican candidate for president, Herbert Hoover, received the electoral votes from all but seven states. After the **Great Depression** began, the tide turned. Many people blamed Hoover and the Republicans for the economic problems of the country.

In the 1932 presidential election, only six states remained Republican. Franklin D. Roosevelt, the Democratic candidate, received the electoral votes from 42 states.

Name: _____ Date: _____

Franklin D. Roosevelt (cont.)

Directions: Complete the following exercises.

Matching

_____ 1. tutor
_____ 2. natural history
_____ 3. Eleanor Roosevelt
_____ 4. polio
_____ 5. The Great Depression

a. Roosevelt's wife
b. a crippling disease
c. a period of economic slowdown during the 1930s
d. study of plants and animals
e. someone who gives private instruction

Fill in the Blanks

1. Franklin Roosevelt's family provided private tutors, and his _____ supervised his education.

2. Franklin enjoyed _____, particularly swimming and hiking.

3. He went on to _____ and then to Columbia Law School in 1904.

4. He was unable to walk without _____.

5. With the help of his wife, Roosevelt remained active behind the scenes until he ran for _____ of New York in 1928.

Critical Thinking

Since his family was wealthy, Roosevelt could have retired and spent the rest of his life as an invalid with servants and nurses to care for him. Instead, he chose an active, productive career. What does that tell you about his character? Give specific details or examples to support your answer.

_____
_____
_____
_____
_____

Constructed Response

What influence did Roosevelt's mother have on his education, decision to marry, and decision to enter politics? Give specific details or examples to support your answer.

_____
_____
_____
_____

UNIT THREE: THE GREAT DEPRESSION

President Roosevelt

When Franklin D. Roosevelt took office on March 4, 1933, more than 13,000,000 people were out of work, banks had failed, and the country was in trouble. Roosevelt immediately called a special session of Congress. To help the country and its people recover, Roosevelt and Congress quickly passed several measures to relieve poverty, reduce **unemployment**, speed economic recovery, and stabilize the banking industry. Roosevelt's "New Deal" programs didn't provide an immediate cure, but they did ease hard times by addressing basic needs and giving new hope to Americans by setting the groundwork for a gradual recovery.

Roosevelt's **domestic** New Deal programs introduced reforms that involved the government directly in national and economic affairs. During the first hundred days of his administration, he passed many new programs including the **Economy Act**, which reduced government salaries and pensions. A new law made low-alcohol beer legal, even though Prohibition was still in effect.

No session of Congress had ever produced so much important legislation. Roosevelt's success was partly due to widespread desperation and partly to his ability as a strong leader.

Roosevelt and his advisors felt it was important that people see him as a strong leader. To minimize his disability, he was seated first at dinners, and his wheelchair was removed before other guests arrived. The press

President Franklin D. Roosevelt

cooperated by not reporting the extent of his physical problems and publishing pictures that showed him standing (which he could do for short periods of time or with the help of a couple of strong men) or seated only in regular chairs. Many people were unaware that he couldn't walk.

Previous presidents had relied heavily on advice from other politicians who belonged to the same political party. Understanding the enormity of the problems facing the nation, Roosevelt turned for advice to a group called the **Brain Trust**—faculty members from Columbia University and Harvard.

Although the Great Depression hadn't ended by the time of the 1936 election, voters stayed with Roosevelt and the Democrats. He received the electoral votes from every state except Maine and Vermont.

When George Washington refused to run for a third term as president, he set a **precedent** that all other presidents followed—until Franklin D. Roosevelt. Not only did Roosevelt run for a third term and win, he was also elected for a fourth term.

Think About It

What if you have been elected president in 1932 during the Great Depression? What would your priorities have been? What types of laws would you have wanted to pass first?

Name: _____   Date: _____

President Roosevelt (cont.)

Directions: Complete the following exercises.

Matching

_____ 1. unemployment

_____ 2. domestic

_____ 3. Economy Act

_____ 4. Brain Trust

_____ 5. precedent

a. composed of faculty members from Columbia University and Harvard

b. not having a job

c. reduced government salaries and pensions

d. something that happened previously that can serve as an example later on

e. refers to the internal policies of a nation

Fill in the Blanks

1. When Franklin D. Roosevelt took office on March 4, 1933, more than _____ people were out of work.

2. Roosevelt's "_____ _____" programs didn't provide an immediate cure for the Depression.

3. A new law made low-alcohol beer legal, even though _____ was still in effect.

4. Although the Great Depression hadn't ended by the time of the _____ election, voters stayed with Roosevelt and the Democrats.

5. Not only did Roosevelt run for a third term and win, he was also elected for a _____ term.

Constructed Response

Why didn't Roosevelt want people to know the extent of his disability? What steps were taken to conceal his disability? Give specific details or examples to support your answer.

_____

_____

_____

_____

_____

Critical Thinking

Do you think there should be a limit to how long a person can hold a political office? Why or why not? On your own paper, give specific details or examples to support your answer.

UNIT THREE: THE GREAT DEPRESSION

Name: _____ Date: _____

You Be the Reporter

Research

Directions: Learn more about the Stock Market Crash of 1929 and the effect it had on families. Imagine that you are a reporter for a newspaper in December 1929. Your boss sent you to write an article about the effects of the stock market crash on one family who lost everything. On the form below, write a news article that includes a headline and an illustration or picture.

Anytown Newspaper

Headline: _____

Article: _____

_____

_____

_____

_____

_____

_____

_____

_____

_____

_____

_____   (Illustration)

_____

_____

_____

_____

_____

_____

Name: _____ Date: _____

The Lame Duck Amendment

The purpose of the Twentieth Amendment, **ratified** in 1933, was to shorten the time between the election and the date when government officials took office.

Under the original Constitution, a new president and vice president took office on March 4 following the November election. If the **incumbent** president and vice president had not been reelected or had decided not to run, they remained in office for four months after the election. The Twentieth Amendment moved that date up to January 20.

Newly elected members of Congress had to wait to take office until the next regular session of Congress began in December of the year following the election—a full 13 months! In the meantime, those who had not run for office or won reelection retained their positions for over a year. With the change, new members of Congress begin their terms on January 3 following the election.

Section 3 states that if the president-elect dies before taking office, the vice president-elect shall become the president.

The amendment also states that if no president has been selected by January 20, the newly elected vice president shall become acting president until a president is chosen.

If neither the president nor vice president has been chosen by January 20, Congress will decide who becomes acting president.

Graphic Organizer

Directions: Complete the vocabulary chart by creating a definition, using the word in a sentence, and drawing an illustration that helps you remember the meaning of the word.

Word	Definition	Illustration
ratified		
	Sentence	

Word	Definition	Illustration
incumbent		
	Sentence	

UNIT THREE: THE GREAT DEPRESSION

Name: _____   Date: _____

Math Facts

Math Calculations

1. In 1933, the minimum wage was set at 40 cents an hour. How much   _____
   would a person earn each week working 10 hours a day, six days a
   week?

2. What would that person's annual income be?   _____

3. The first parking meter was installed in Oklahoma City, Oklahoma, in   _____
   1935. How many years ago was that?

4. There were 750 miles of paved roads in the United States in 1909. By   _____
   1930, that number had gone up to 100,000 miles. On average, how
   many miles of road would have had to have been built per year during
   that 21-year time period? Round your answer to the nearest mile.

5. The world-famous Mickey Mouse™ watch first became available in   _____
   1933. It sold for $2.75. At 40 cents an hour, how long would a person
   have to work to pay for a Mickey Mouse™ watch? Round your answer
   to the nearest hour.

6. In 1937, wages for workers at U.S. Steel were raised to $5 a day. How   _____
   much did they earn per hour if they worked ten-hour days?

7. The U.S. Treasury Department announced in October 1925 that they   _____
   had fined 29,620 people for Prohibition (alcohol) violations. The fines
   totaled $5,000,000. What was the average amount of fine per person?
   Round your answer to the nearest dollar.

8. Herbert Hoover's first job after college was as a pick-and-shovel miner   _____
   for $2.50 a day. How much did he earn for a six-day workweek?

9. The first MONOPOLY™ games sold for $4 each. Working with a friend,   _____
   Charles Darrow could make six games a day. How much would they
   have taken in if they had sold all the games they made in 15 days?

10. In 1924, a Ford Model T sold for $290. The Model A introduced in 1927   _____
    sold for $395. What was the percent of increase in the cost? Round
    your answer to the nearest percent.

11. In 1920, less than 15 percent of the people in the United States   _____
    had a telephone. The population of the United States in 1920 was
    105,710,620. What would be 15 percent of that number?

12. By 1930, the population of the United States had risen to 122,775,046.   _____
    How many more people were there than in 1920?

96

Name: _____   Date: _____

The Repeal of Prohibition

The Eighteenth Amendment prohibiting alcohol was ratified by voters in three-quarters of the states, yet no law was ever so violently opposed and ignored at all levels of American society. As a result, many people felt Prohibition promoted disrespect for the law.

Almost as soon as Prohibition was passed, people began working to repeal it. They felt that the law was an invasion of the private lives of citizens. Another argument for repeal was that Prohibition generated organized crime and that the profits that could be made from illegal alcohol promoted corruption at almost every level of government.

In 1933, Section 1 of the Twenty-First Amendment to the Constitution ended Prohibition. According to Section 2, if any state, territory, or possession of the United States wanted to make alcohol illegal, they had the right to do so. It would then be illegal to import or manufacture alcohol in those areas.

Graphic Organizer

Directions: Research the Era of Prohibition. Create a time line of five important events from 1830 to 1933 related to the prohibition of alcohol. Include the date and the name of the event and a brief description.

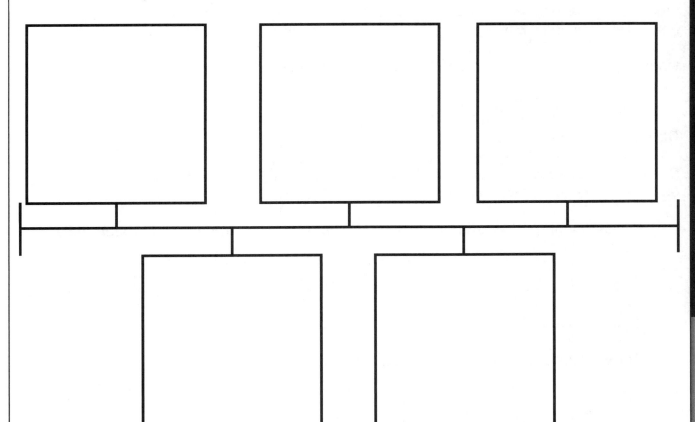

UNIT THREE: THE GREAT DEPRESSION

Name: _____   Date: _____

Isolationism

During much of its history, the United States has maintained an **isolationist** policy, believing the country's best interest would be served by avoiding alliances with other nations.

This policy of isolationism kept the United States out of World War I until 1917. When the United States finally declared war, leaders felt our country was obligated to "make the world safe for democracy."

After World War I, President Woodrow Wilson presented a plan for a general association of nations that became the League of Nations in 1920. Although Wilson was a member of the committee that drafted the charter, the U.S. Senate never ratified it.

Article X of the charter stated that if any nation threatened a member country, all members of the league would be obligated to help, even if it meant war.

American diplomats encouraged the league's activities and unofficially attended meetings, but the United States never became a member of the League of Nations.

World War I was called "the war to end all wars." However, it soon became clear that all countries would not be democracies, and nations would continue to fight wars. Faced with the problems of the Great Depression, the tendency toward isolationism increased. Many people decided to ignore the problems in other countries, choosing rather to focus on and solve problems at home.

During the 1930s, new dictators came to power in Germany, Japan, Italy, and Russia, causing a flood of immigration to the United States. Instead of welcoming new arrivals, Congress cut the number of immigrants allowed in an effort to control and restrict foreign influences.

In the early thirties, Congress also voted to restrict foreign trade to protect the U.S. economy and to remain neutral in foreign disputes.

Cause and Effect

Directions: A cause is an event that produces a result. An effect is the result produced. For each cause, write a possible effect.

1. **Cause:** During the 1930s, new dictators came to power in Germany, Japan, Italy, and Russia.

   Effect: _____

   _____

2. **Cause:** The Great Depression increased isolationism.

   Effect: _____

   _____

Name: _____   Date: _____

New Deal Programs

One popular New Deal program was the **Civilian Conservation Corps (CCC)**. Established by Congress in 1933, the CCC provided needy young men with jobs in forests and national parks.

The program had two main purposes: employment and training for young men and conservation of natural resources including timber, soil, and water. Unemployed, unmarried men between the ages of 17 and 23 were eligible to join the CCC. They were paid $30 a month and lived in work camps. About three million men were employed by the CCC.

Workers carved out roads and hiking trails, cleaned up beaches, and cleared camping sites to develop national parks. They laid down telephone lines and constructed fire observation towers. Reforestation projects included planting about two million trees from Texas to North Dakota.

The **Works Progress Administration (WPA)** began in 1935 when the president and Congress decided to shift federal relief funds to providing useful employment. By 1943, the program had provided jobs for nine million workers in road maintenance and construction of buildings and facilities. The **National Youth Administration (NYA)** program also provided four million part-time jobs.

Projects included the construction of schools, dormitories, hospitals, airports, docks, and ports, plus slum clearance, flood control, and rural electrification. The WPA also provided jobs for artists (painting murals on public buildings), writers (conducting research projects), and actors and actresses (touring and performing in rural areas) through the Federal Writers, Theater, and Arts Program.

Graphic Organizer

Directions: Using the Venn diagram, compare the Civilian Conservation Corps (CCC) to the Works Progress Administration (WPA).

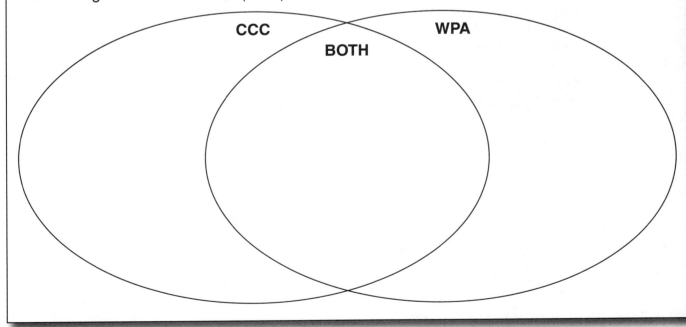

UNIT THREE: THE GREAT DEPRESSION

Name: _____ Date: _____

An Alphabet Soup of New Deal Programs

Besides the **CCC**, the **WPA**, and the **NYA**, Roosevelt's New Deal included a whole alphabet soup of other programs. Even Roosevelt himself was often referred to as **FDR**.

Research

Directions: Research New Deal programs to answer the questions about the following acronyms.

One of Roosevelt's earliest concerns was to stabilize banks and give depositors a sense of security. The **FDIC** insured the savings of depositors up to $5,000 at all Federal Reserve banks.

1. What did **FDIC** stand for? _____

The **TVA** was authorized to manage local resources and construct a series of hydroelectric dams to provide cheap power.

2. What did **TVA** stand for? _____

Created in 1933, **FERA** granted three billion dollars to states to fund work projects for unemployed adults.

3. What did **FERA** stand for? _____

The **AAA** provided crop reduction subsidies to stabilize prices and loans for overdue farm mortgages.

4. What did **AAA** stand for? _____

Another federal program, the **HOLC**, helped people in danger of losing their homes due to foreclosure by allowing them to refinance with low-interest loans.

5. What did **HOLC** stand for? _____

The **NRA** was designed to assist industry and labor by establishing voluntary codes and standards for wages, working hours, child labor, etc. As a whole, this program had many faults, but it did bring about shorter workdays and five-day workweeks.

6. What did **NRA** stand for? (Note: this was not the National Rifle Association.)

_____

Desperate Times, Desperate People, Desperate Actions

When the International Apple Shippers Association came up with an **oversupply** of fruit in 1930, they also came up with a unique solution. They sold apples on **credit** to people who were unemployed. The unemployed stood on street corners selling apples for five cents each.

This trend led to others besides apple sellers **peddling** everything from watches to patent medicines. Cities eventually had to pass laws banning street vendors as a public nuisance.

People who were desperate sometimes turned to pawnshops. In exchange for a ring, watch, or other treasured item, **pawnshops** might loan a person a few dollars to buy groceries, pay the rent, or keep the car from being repossessed. If people could not repay the loan plus interest in a certain amount of time, the pawnshop would keep their items and resell them for a profit.

In March 1933, about 1,000 people a day all across the country lost their homes due to foreclosures. When people couldn't pay their rent or mortgages, they were evicted from their homes.

Desperate for places to live, people moved into abandoned factories and warehouses. Shanty towns called **Hoovervilles** sprang up in empty lots, under bridges, in city dumps, and along major highways.

People scrounged through city dumps, construction sites, and trash bins for materials to build shelters. Abandoned cars and stacks of wooden fruit boxes became homes for desperate families. They lacked electricity and running water. Crime, disease, and hunger filled these shanty towns.

Those who managed to keep or find jobs often had to take a cut in pay and/or a cut in hours. People took in boarders to help pay the bills and share expenses. Women and children worked when they could. People begged when they had no other choice.

Blacks and immigrants were affected as much or more by the lack of jobs. Often the last hired and the first fired, they earned less, worked harder, and had less job security even in good times. Blacks who had been tenant farmers in the South migrated to the North hoping to find work.

Did You Know?

Reading became a popular form of entertainment during the thirties. Penguin Books, launched in England in 1935, pioneered the "paperback revolution" by publishing inexpensive classics and new novels.

UNIT THREE: THE GREAT DEPRESSION

Name: _____ Date: _____

Desperate Times, Desperate People, Desperate Actions (cont.)

Directions: Complete the following exercises.

Matching

_____ 1. oversupply

_____ 2. credit

_____ 3. peddling

_____ 4. pawnshops

_____ 5. Hoovervilles

    a. provide funds or money in exchange for an item

    b. selling items on street corners

    c. shanty towns named for Herbert Hoover

    d. more of an item than is needed

    e. to buy an item with a promise of later payment

Fill in the Blanks

1. The unemployed stood on street corners selling _____ for five cents each.

2. Cities eventually had to pass laws banning _____ _____ as a public nuisance.

3. In March 1933, about 1,000 people a day all across the country lost their homes due to _____.

4. People scrounged through city dumps, construction sites, and trash bins for materials to build _____.

5. Those who managed to keep or find _____ often had to take a cut in pay and/or a cut in hours.

Constructed Response

How did the Apple Shippers Association's solution help the Association, consumers, and the unemployed? Give specific details or examples to support your answer.

_____

_____

_____

_____

_____

_____

_____

_____

_____

_____

UNIT THREE: THE GREAT DEPRESSION

George W. Norris

George William Norris was born in Ohio in 1861. He was one of the greatest statesmen in the history of American public life. His hallmark was independence. As a congressman, he never hesitated to put his own political party far behind the national interest—even if it meant **censure** from his colleagues.

He studied at Valparaiso University in Indiana. When he was 24, he moved to Nebraska. Norris was first elected to the U.S. House of Representatives in 1902—during the high point of the **Progressive Movement**.

In 1910, when House **insurgents** attempted to challenge the power of Speaker of the House Joseph Cannon, Norris led the campaign. Despite every attempt by the wily Cannon to oppose the changes in House rules, Norris won the day, thus paving the way for **fundamental** reforms.

In 1912, Norris was elected a United States senator from Nebraska. In 1917, when the issue of America's entrance into the war was at hand, Norris led a brief but futile fight to keep the country out of Europe's troubles. After the war, Norris opposed U.S. entry into the League of Nations, thinking that American participation would lead the nation into more wars.

Norris's great interest was in the extension of publicly owned utilities. Muscle Shoals, the great dam in Alabama, had been built during the war to provide cheap electricity for farmers. During the years of the Harding-Coolidge administration (1921–1925), there were numerous attempts by private enterprises to obtain control of the dam. Norris opposed them all, even blocking the lease of the project to Henry Ford for $5 million.

What Norris really wanted was to incorporate the Muscle Shoals Dam into a larger complex of proposed dams on the Tennessee River. Opposed by his own Republican Party,

Norris led the fight in 1933 to establish the **Tennessee Valley Authority**.

In time, the TVA built 30 dams on the Tennessee and its tributaries. Nine of the high dams created huge man-made lakes, such as Kentucky Lake, and provided electrical power to poor regions. Parks were created, trees and grass were planted over eroded areas, soil fertility was restored—these, and a new way of life, were by-products of TVA.

It is somewhat important to understand that Norris did not come from Appalachia. He came from Nebraska—some distance away. As a salute to his efforts, one of the dams on the Tennessee was named after him.

Norris also helped to enact the Twentieth Amendment to the Constitution. In the late 1930s, Norris realized the dangers of the spread of fascism in Europe, and gave his support for aid to Great Britain. It may have been this factor that led to his defeat for the Senate in 1942.

Name: _____ Date: _____

George W. Norris (cont.)

Directions: Complete the following exercises.

Matching

_____ 1. censure
_____ 2. Progressive Movement
_____ 3. insurgents
_____ 4. fundamental
_____ 5. Tennessee Valley Authority

a. era of reform in America
b. New Deal program to build dams
c. basic
d. rebellious people
e. to be reprimanded or rebuked

Fill in the Blanks

1. Norris was one of the greatest _____ in the history of public life.

2. In 1912, Norris was elected a United States _____ from _____.

3. Norris's great interest was in the extension of publicly owned _____.

4. In time, the TVA built _____ _____ on the Tennessee River and its tributaries.

5. Norris also helped to enact the _____ Amendment to the Constitution.

Constructed Response

What were some benefits of the TVA building dams on the Tennessee River and its tributaries? Give specific details or examples to support your answer.

_____

_____

_____

_____

_____

Critical Thinking

Do you think George Norris was "one of the greatest statesmen in the history of American public life"? Why or why not? Give specific details or examples to support your opinion.

_____

_____

_____

_____

UNIT THREE: THE GREAT DEPRESSION

Name: _____ Date: _____

Let's Listen to the Radio

After the stock market crash of 1929, radio broadcasting was one of the few businesses that prospered during hard times. With millions out of work and money for recreation scarce, radio provided cheap entertainment. Radio also brought people from different classes and different parts of the country together in a new way. Farmers in Iowa could listen to the same music as party-goers in New York. A poor woman in Mississippi could enjoy the same radio adventures as a rich man in California.

Besides live music and records, people listened to political speeches, sports programs, and weather forecasts. Franklin D. Roosevelt kept Americans informed with a series of "fireside chats" to encourage people that the situation in the country was gradually improving.

Radio also brought situation comedies and dramas into the homes of millions of Americans. Soap operas dominated the daytime airwaves. The most popular program of the thirties was "Amos 'n' Andy," which attracted as many as 30 million listeners each week.

Other popular serials were "Fibber McGee and Molly," "Little Orphan Annie," "The Green Hornet," "The Shadow," "Jack Armstrong, All-American Boy," "Dick Tracy," and "The Lone Ranger." Many radio stars like Jack Benny went on to make names for themselves in movies and TV.

Did You Know?
The presidential inauguration was broadcast on radio for the first time when Calvin Coolidge took the oath of office in Washington, D.C., in March 1925.

In radio, a person's voice and personality were important, but how they looked didn't matter. The audience could imagine the character any way they wished, based on what they heard.

Besides providing entertainment and information, radio also broadcast advertisements. Even if people couldn't afford new products, they could listen to descriptions—and dream of the day when their lives might be better.

One illustration of the impact radio had on Americans was the October 30, 1938, broadcast of the science fiction play "War of the Worlds" about the invasion of Martians. A million listeners panicked as they mistook the play for a newscast.

UNIT THREE: THE GREAT DEPRESSION

Constructed Response

Besides music, list five other types of radio programming people listened to in the 1930s.

_____

_____

_____

_____

Name: _____ Date: _____

Eleanor Roosevelt

Research
Directions: Research the life of Eleanor Roosevelt to fill in the blanks.

Eleanor Roosevelt became the most active first lady to live in the White House up to that time.

1. Although she grew up in a wealthy family, Eleanor Roosevelt's childhood must have been far from happy. When she was eight years old, her _____ died, and she went to live with her _____ _____, a very stern woman.

2. Eleanor was deeply attached to her father, an alcoholic who was often away for treatments and was seldom allowed to visit her. He died when she was _____ years old.

3. Eleanor was sent to a boarding school in _____ when she was 15.

4. Long before her husband, _____, was elected president, Eleanor had been an active woman, interested in politics and social conditions. She did charity work in Albany, New York, and worked for the Red Cross during World War I.

5. Unlike most previous first ladies, Eleanor Roosevelt did not believe in staying quietly in the background. She traveled extensively visiting hospitals and schools, held weekly press conferences, and wrote articles and a newspaper column titled, "_____."

6. Eleanor seemed to enjoy adventure. At the Winter Olympics at _____, New York, she took a ride down the bobsled run. On her way to the Democratic National Convention in 1940, the pilot let her fly the plane.

7. Never one to back away from controversial issues, Eleanor took a stand when members of the Daughters of the American Revolution prevented Marian Anderson, a black singer, from performing at Constitution Hall in Washington, D.C., in 1939. Angrily, Eleanor resigned from the group and organized an alternate site for the concert at the _____ _____.

8. Eleanor remained active after her husband's death and became the U.S. delegate to the _____ from 1945 to 1953.

9. What was Eleanor Roosevelt's maiden name? _____

10. Who was her famous uncle? _____

Name: _____   Date: _____

The Social Security Act of 1935

Another important law passed while Franklin Roosevelt was president was the Social Security Act of 1935. This act set up six specific programs and established methods of taxes to fund them.

Old-Age Benefits (later called Social Security) was funded by federal taxes deducted from workers. When workers retired at age 65, they became eligible to receive a monthly check. Benefits were extended to widows and dependent children of retired workers.

States taxed employers to fund the **Unemployment Compensation** program, providing income to people who were out of work.

The other four programs were forms of welfare funded by grants from the federal government and administered by the states. They included **Old-Age Assistance**, **Aid to Dependent Children**, **Maternal and Child Welfare**, and **Aid to the Blind**.

Old-Age Assistance and Aid to the Blind programs were designed to supplement Old-Age Benefits or to provide benefits for those not eligible for Old-Age Benefits.

Maternal and Child Welfare provided health care to poor mothers and their children and was designed to protect and care for homeless, neglected, or disabled children. Aid to Dependent Children helped support children living with only one parent or with relatives other than parents.

The first Social Security cards were issued in 1937 when the government began collecting Social Security taxes. Each person received a unique number used to keep track of earnings and taxes paid. Money was placed into a trust fund to be used to pay benefits, cover the costs of administering the program, and earn interest to build up the fund. To build up the fund, people who retired before 1940 received only one lump sum payment rather than monthly benefits.

Graphic Organizer

Directions: Complete the vocabulary chart by creating a definition, using the word in a sentence, and drawing an illustration that helps you remember the meaning of the word.

Word	Definition	Illustration
compensation		
	Sentence	
Word	Definition	Illustration
dependent		
	Sentence	

UNIT THREE: THE GREAT DEPRESSION

Name: _____ Date: _____

The Dust Bowl

Life had always been difficult for home-steaders on the Great Plains. Farms were small and water scarce with no reservoirs or irrigation systems. Even in good years, many were lucky to break even.

Before farmers moved to the area in the late 1800s, the land was covered with hardy grasses that held the fine-grained soil in place even during times of drought, wind, or heavy rains.

When large numbers of homesteaders settled in the region, they plowed up the grass-es and planted crops. The cattle they raised ate whatever grass was left. This exposed the soil to the winds that constantly swept across the flat plains. When a series of droughts hit the area in the early thirties, combined with the farming practices of the past 50 years, there was nothing to hold the soil in place.

A large area in the southern part of the Great Plains region of the United States came to be known as the **Dust Bowl** during the 1930s. Much of this area suffered extensively from soil erosion.

The Depression had already caused the price of wheat and corn to fall to all-time lows. When crops failed, farmers couldn't make

mortgage payments on their farms. By 1932, a thousand families a week were losing their farms in Texas, Oklahoma, and Arkansas. Thousands of families migrated west in search of a better life.

In 1935, both the federal and state governments began developing programs to conserve the soil and reclaim the area. This included seeding large areas with grass; the rotation of wheat, then sorghum, and then ly-ing fallow; contour plowing; terracing; and strip planting. In some areas, "shelter belts" of trees were planted to break the force of the wind.

Cause and Effect

Directions: For the cause listed below, write a possible effect.

Cause: The Dust Bowl, the Great Depression, and crop failure led to families losing their farms in Texas, Oklahoma, and Arkansas.

Effect: _____

_____

Research

Directions: Learn more about one of the methods for conserving the soil or reclaiming the land listed in the last paragraph of the reading exercise. On poster board, create an illustration of how the technique works and how it can prevent soil loss.

Name: _____ Date: _____

Conditions Get Worse

The problems in the Dust Bowl area increased in 1936 when the winds began blowing almost continuously. People fled to shelter as huge clouds of dust advanced on them. Dust was carried great distances by the wind, in some cases darkening the sky all the way to the Atlantic Ocean.

During the next four years, as much as three to four inches of topsoil blew away, leaving only hard, red clay, which made farming impossible. Sand settled around homes, fences, and barns. People slept with wet cloths over their faces to filter out the dust. They woke to find themselves, their pillows, and blankets caked with dirt. Animals were buried alive or choked to death on the dust.

People died if they remained outside too long during a dust storm. Many also died from what came to be called "dust pneumonia"—severe damage to the lungs caused by breathing dust.

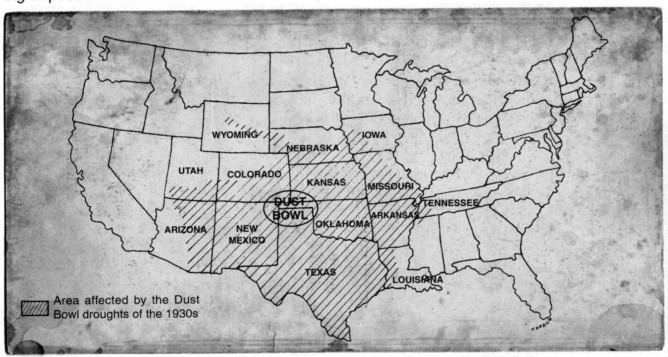

Area affected by the Dust Bowl droughts of the 1930s

Map Skills

1. Centered in northern Texas, the panhandle of Oklahoma, and southwestern Kansas, the Dust Bowl also included all or part of which other states?

   _____

   _____

   _____

2. Which four states were completely in the area affected by the Dust Bowl?

   _____

3. Which three states in the area affected by the Dust Bowl were farthest north?

   _____

Name: _____   Date: _____

A Cottage for Sale

Music in the thirties reflected both pessimism due to economic conditions and optimism for a better time to come. People listened to upbeat songs like "Bye, Bye Blues," "Sunny Side Up," and "Get Happy" as well as songs with more serious themes, like "Brother, Can You Spare a Dime?"

Word Search Puzzle
Directions: Words from **"A Cottage for Sale,"** recorded by Guy Lombardo in 1930, can be found in the puzzle. (At that time a cottage meant a small house, not a vacation place.) Look up, down, backward, forward, and diagonally to find and circle the words printed in bold.

Our **little dream castle** with **every** dream **gone**,
is **lonely and silent**, the **shades** are all **drawn**,
and my **heart** is **heavy** as I **gaze upon**
A **cottage** for **sale**.

The **lawn** we were **proud** of is **waving** in **hay**,
Our **beautiful garden** has **withered away**,
Where **you planted roses**, the **weeds seem** to **say**,
A cottage for sale.

From every **single window**, I **see** your **face**,
But when I reach a window, there's **empty space**,
The key's in the **mail** box the same as **before**,
But no one is **waiting any more**,
The **end** of the **story** is **told** on the **door**,
A cottage for sale.

```
B Y N F E C A P S L I A M A D
E E A W A N O G N I V A W E R
F S A S A C O T T Z E A T E A
O A T U S L E G T R Y N Z Y W
R L I T T L E D D A A A L V N
E E L G N I S K E L G E Y A H
S E S O R T F D P R N E H E W
H T V O N O P U J O E S N H O
A Z O E R O M O L Y E H D D D
D D L R R G A R D E N L T N N
E I U O Y Y T P M E O A A I I
S D E E W V V W A I T I N G U W
```

Name: _____ Date: _____

The Thirties: Cause and Effect

Directions: A **cause** is an event that produces a result. An **effect** is the result produced. For each cause, write a possible effect.

Cause	Effect

Cause

Effect

1. Banks across the country closed after the stock market crashed.

_____

_____

_____

2. Parts of the country experienced a drought for several years.

_____

_____

_____

3. Millions of people were unemployed during the thirties.

_____

_____

_____

4. Eleanor Roosevelt was a very active first lady.

_____

_____

_____

5. Congress set up work programs like the CCC and WPA.

_____

_____

_____

6. The Lame Duck Amendment changed the date new members of Congress took office.

_____

_____

_____

Name: _____   Date: _____

Thirties Internet Scavenger Hunt

Technology in the Classroom
Directions: Search the Internet to locate the answers to the scavenger hunt questions below.

Herbert Hoover's vice president, Charles Curtis, was a Native American.

1. To what tribe did he belong? _____

In 1930, this baseball great signed a two-year contract with the New York Yankees for the huge sum of $80,000.

2. Who was he? _____

An actor who later became a national political figure made his movie debut in 1937 when he was 26 years old in the Warner Brothers movie *Love is in the Air.*

3. What was his name? _____

In May 1932, Public Enemy Number One, Al Capone, was sent to the Atlanta Penitentiary.

4. Of what crime was he convicted? _____

The first episode of "The Lone Ranger" was heard on radio in 1933 and ran until 1954. Several different radio actors played the part of the Lone Ranger, including Clayton Moore from 1949 to 1952. The part of his faithful companion, Tonto, was played for almost the entire time by John Todd, a bald Irishman. On radio and later on television and in films, every episode of "The Lone Ranger" began with the same music.

5. What was the name of the song?

_____

6. Who played Tonto after it became a TV show?

_____

Before the "Singing Cowboy" became famous in movies in the thirties, he worked as a telegraph operator. He made more than 90 Westerns during his career and had a TV show that ran for six seasons.

7. Who was the "Singing Cowboy"? _____

Fred Waring invented the Waring Blender. However, he was more famous for his other occupation.

8. What was Fred Waring's occupation? _____

Band leader and clarinetist Artie Shaw became famous in the thirties.

9. What was Artie Shaw's real name? _____

Name: _____   Date: _____

Review the Thirties

Matching

Directions: Match each word to its definition. Use the Internet or reference sources if you need help.

_____ 1. reservoir

_____ 2. erosion

_____ 3. bankrupt

_____ 4. Social Security Act

_____ 5. Lame Duck Amendment

_____ 6. irrigation

_____ 7. drought

_____ 8. Civilian Conservation Corps

a. Provided jobs for young, unemployed single men

b. A system used to carry water to where it is needed for crops

c. A long period of time with little or no rain

d. A place to hold surplus water for later use

e. Broke; having no money; unable to pay debts

f. Provided Old-Age Benefits

g. Wearing away of soil due to wind or rain

h. Changed date of presidential inauguration

True or False

Directions: Circle "T" for True or "F" for False.

1. T F Isolationism is a disease that causes people to sleep a lot.

2. T F Franklin D. Roosevelt was elected president four times.

3. T F The thirties were called the Great Depression Era because most people were sad during those years.

4. T F The Dust Bowl was an annual football game played between the top two college teams in Texas.

5. T F Franklin D. Roosevelt was a Democrat.

6. T F During the Depression, people were often hungry. To show they had no food, they put empty bowls on the table and called them Dust Bowls.

7. T F Many flourishing cities were named Hooverville or Hoovertown in honor of Herbert Hoover.

8. T F Many of Roosevelt's New Deal programs were aimed at helping those who were unemployed.

9. T F MONOPOLY™ was invented by a rich businessman.

10. T F Radio brought music, news, weather, sports, dramas, comedies, and soap operas into millions of homes during the Depression.

UNIT THREE: THE GREAT DEPRESSION

Name: _____ Date: _____

Then and Now

Directions: Read the statements about conditions during the Great Depression. Add a statement about conditions today.

1. **Then:** Millions of people were unemployed.

   Now: _____

   _____

   _____

2. **Then:** Millions of people were homeless.

   Now: _____

   _____

   _____

3. **Then:** Listening to the radio and going to the movies were favorite pastimes.

   Now: _____

   _____

   _____

4. **Then:** MONOPOLY™ and Scrabble™ were popular board games. Children enjoyed playing with dolls, toy cars, blocks, and toy planes.

   Now: _____

   _____

   _____

5. **Then:** People enjoyed listening to jazz and dancing to Big Band music.

   Now: _____

   _____

   _____

6. **Then:** Franklin D. Roosevelt was president.

   Now: _____

   _____

   _____

Learn More About ...

Technology in the Classroom

Directions: Learn more about one of the people listed below who had an impact on American history during the Roaring Twenties and/or the Great Depression Era. Using the information, create a multimedia biography presentation. Be sure to include text, photographs, audio, and/or video in your presentation. Share your presentation with the class.

Charles Lindbergh

Amelia Earhart

Marian Anderson
Louis Armstrong
Pearl S. Buck
Richard Byrd
Al Capone
Charlie Chaplin
Calvin Coolidge
Douglas Corrigan
Charles Coughlin
Walt Disney
Isadora Duncan
Amelia Earhart
Duke Ellington
Edna Ferber
Henry Ford
George Gershwin
Benny Goodman
Woody Guthrie
Warren G. Harding
Ernest Hemingway
Herbert Hoover

Harry Houdini
Sinclair Lewis
Charles Lindbergh
Huey Long
Amy Lowell
Margaret Mead
Jelly Roll Morton
Jesse Owens
Frances Perkins
Will Rogers
Eleanor Roosevelt
Franklin D. Roosevelt
Nellie Tayloe Ross
Florence Sabin
Margaret Sanger
Upton Sinclair
Bessie Smith
Gertrude Stein
John Steinbeck
Francis Townsend
Rudolph Valentino

Walt Disney

Rudolph Valentino

Isadora Duncan

UNIT THREE: THE GREAT DEPRESSION

Answer Keys

Only exercises with definite answers are listed in the answer keys.

Unit One: Industrialization
Industrialization Time Line Activity (p. 2)
1. Eli Whitney invents the cotton gin.
2. The Erie Canal is completed.
3. Thomas Newcomen builds his first steam engine.
4. James Hargreaves develops the spinning jenny.
5. Samuel Slater opens the first working U.S. cotton mill.
6. Work began on the Erie Canal.
7. Isaac Singer produces the first successful sewing machine.
8. A New York department store installs the first safety elevator.
9. Thomas Edison invents the phonograph.
10. Alexander Graham Bell invents the telephone.

Fill in the Blanks
1. George Westinghouse
2. dynamo
3. typewriter
4. Thomas Newcomen
5. Bessemer
6. automobiles

Water Power (p. 5)
A. sluice
B. buckets
C. grinding stones
D. stream
E. wheel
F. shaft
G. gears
H. flour

Eli Whitney's Solutions (p. 9)
Graphic Organizer
Solution #1: Use interchangeable parts.
Solution #2: Design machines that unskilled workers could use.
Solution #3: Whitney gave a demonstration that proved his idea worked.

How Do You Make Clothes? (p. 11)
Constructed Response
3. 6, 1, 3, 2, 5, 4

Eli Whitney's Cotton Gin (p. 12)
Cause and Effect
(Answers may vary. Possible answers are given.)
Growing cotton soon became profitable.
Plantation owners wanted more slaves so they could grow even more cotton.
Both young and old people who were not strong enough to work at other types of jobs started to work ginning cotton.
People paid their debts, and land increased in value.
Factories in the North started to use the cotton to make cloth.
The shipping industry grew.

Early American Factories (p. 14)
Matching
1. e   2. b   3. c   4. d   5. a
Fill in the Blanks
1. Samuel Slater   2. children   3. day
4. sunrise, sunset   5. waterwheel
True or False
1. F   2. T   3. F   4. T   5. T
Constructed Response
Children were already working long hours on their family farms.

The First True Steam Engine (p. 18)
A. wooden rocking beam   B. connecting chain
C. cylinder   D. boiler   E. fire
F. pump rods   G. mine shaft

Learning Steam Power Terms (p. 20)
Vocabulary
1. steam: the vapor that is formed when water boils
2. condenser: an apparatus in which steam is condensed back into water
3. boiler: a tank that is heated to turn water into steam
4. engine: a machine that changes an energy source into movement
5. piston: a disc or cylinder that moves back and forth in a large cylinder; steam engines have pistons. Their back-and-forth movement is converted to rotational movement.
6. rotary motion: turning on an axis like a wheel
7. governor: an attachment to a machine for automatic control or limitation of speed

Water Power vs. Steam Power (p. 21)
Graphic Organizer
1. No   2. No   3. Yes   4. Yes
5. Yes   6. Yes   7. No   8. Yes
9. No   10. Yes   11. Yes

Robert Fulton (p. 23)
Fill in the Blanks
1. steamboat   2. flax   3. paddles
4. everyday   5. financed
True or False
1. T   2. T   3. T   4. F   5. F
Constructed Response
1. After several years of bad weather, the family was forced to sell their farm and move back to Lancaster where Robert's father ran a successful tailoring shop. Two years later, however, Robert Fulton, Sr., died. Then Robert Fulton became quite ill. He went

to Europe where he hoped to improve his health and become an even better painter.
2. The Industrial Revolution was underway. Fulton studied new inventions and met with inventors.

Critical Thinking
Answers will vary, but might include: They did not want other countries to be able to compete with British manufacturing.

Canals (p. 24)
1. A canal is a channel for water that is dug across land.
2. Canals were built to connect bodies of water so that barges or ships could travel between them.
3. As the horses walked a path running alongside the canal, they towed freight and passenger barges.
4. Horses
5. The hoggees were the men who drove the teams that pulled the canal boats.
6. A cobbler is someone who makes or repairs shoes.
7. Hoggees would wear out their shoes as they walked along the canal.
8. Canals and rivers often froze until spring.
9. Most roads then were unpaved and muddy.
10. A lock is a part of a canal with gates at each end where boats are raised or lowered to different water levels.

DeWitt Clinton (p. 26)
Fill in the Blanks
1. West   2. 363   3. Hudson River
4. senator, mayor, governor   5. $7,000,000

Time Line
A. 3   B. 2   C. 1   D. 4

Cause and Effect
In any order: began a wave of canal construction; speeded up immigration to the West; reduced the cost of transportation

The Erie Canal (p. 27)
Teacher check map.

Fascinating Facts About the Erie Canal (p. 28)
1. 1817   2. farmers   3. Ireland
4. one dollar   5. 85   6. Lake Erie
7. eastern   8. cities   9. Mills
10. immigration   11. west   12. Freight
13. Buffalo   14. deep   15. wide
16. tolls   17. thousands   18. hoggees
19. hostellers   20. steam trains

All About Iron (p. 31)
1. Stone, bone, wood, bronze
2. They would fall apart, bend, or break.
3. Iron tools were hard and would last.
4. Iron ore is a natural rock that contains iron.
5. Iron
6. Large buildings
7. The machines were large and operated by belts from an overhead shaft. They needed huge, open floor areas for production and storage.

Taller and Taller Buildings (p. 32)
Internet Scavenger Hunt
1. Crystal Palace   2. Eiffel Tower
3. Home Insurance Building   4. 57 stories
5. 1,250 feet or 381 meters
6. 1,450 feet or 442 meters
7. 1,821 feet or 550 meters
8. 1,483 feet or 452 meters
9. 2,717 feet or 828 meters; 162 stories

Inventing a Safe Elevator (p. 33)
Fill in the Blanks
1. New York City   2. standard-sized
3. mass-produced   4. hoists
5. cables   6. stairs
7. Otis   8. safety mechanism
9. elevator   10. World's Fair
11. cut   12. possible

How Did Steam Locomotives Affect America? (p. 34)
All answers +

Morse Code (p. 36)
Decoding
1. SOS   2. Goodbye

Alike and Different (p. 37)
Graphic Organizer
Samuel Morse only: early interest in electricity; born in 1791
Robert Fulton only: early interest in finding new ways to complete tasks; born in 1765
Both: invented several things; persevered; studied art in Europe; experienced hardships

A History of Electricity (p. 39)
1. Lightning frightened many people.
2. The Netherlands is a small country in Europe.
3. Those sparks were amazing.
4. Electricity was an interesting subject.
5. I wonder why it took so long.
6. Edison also invented the phonograph.

Learning Electricity Terms (p. 40)
Matching
1. e   2. f   3. g   4. c   5. a   6. b
7. h   8. d

How Does Electricity Affect the Earth? (p. 41)
1. coal
2. steam
3. generators
4. carbon dioxide
5. increasing
6. heat
7. greenhouse
8. reduce
9. fossil
10. energy
11. Nuclear
12. lttireeciyc   13. electricity

Thomas Alva Edison (p. 43)
Time Line Activity
A. 8   B. 9   C. 2   D. 7   E. 4   F. 10
G. 5   H. 1   I. 3   J. 6

True or False
1. F   2. F   3. T   4. F   5. T

Thomas Edison Crossword Puzzle (p. 44)

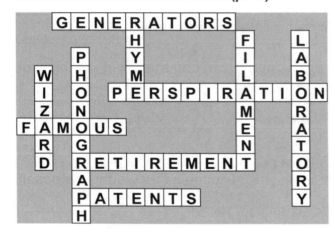

One Thing Affects Another (p. 45)
1. Effect: The coal industry boomed.
2. Cause: The coal industry needed trains and rails made of high-quality steel. Technology that produced high-quality steel became available.
3. Cause: There were many new railroads.
   Effect: The mail delivery was speeded up.
4. Effects: Americans could order products from distant cities. Newspapers could report news from across the nation. Railroad engineers could find out the exact locations of trains.

Get the Message? (p. 46)
2. What hath God wrought!
6. That's one small step for man, one giant leap for mankind.

Hello, How Are You? (p. 47)
A. 3 B. 10 C. 2 D. 8 E. 7 F. 9
G. 6 H. 5 I. 1 J. 4 K. 11

Henry Ford and the Assembly Line (p. 50)
Constructed Response
Ford simplified the design and production of the Model T by the assembly-line process. By doing so, he reduced the price of the auto from $950 to $290.

Industrial Mathematics (p. 52)
Math Calculations
1. $\frac{1}{4}$ 2. $\frac{1}{2}$ 3. 35 years   4. 360
5. 48,000 6. 580   7. 35,000   8. 18 years
9. $490 10. 719,000

Power Statements (p. 53)
True or False
1. T   2. F   3. F   4. F   5. T   6. F   7. T
8. T   9. F   10. T   11. T   12. T   13. T   14. F

Cool Facts (p. 55)
Cooperative Learning
1. two
2. 363
3. Otis
4. Madam Curie
5. hammer
6. 1.3 million
7. television
8. black and white
9. big
10. black
11. 1958
12. Triangle Shirtwaist Factory

Business Grows in Size and Influence (p. 57)
Constructed Response
1. A & P (Atlantic and Pacific) stores
2. unskilled labor
3. Alexander Hamilton's

Captains of Industry or Robber Barons (60)
Time Line Activity
A. 6   B. 9   C. 5   D. 4   E. 7   F. 2
G. 3   H. 8   I. 1

Graphic Organizer
Cornelius Vanderbilt: railroads
Gustavus Swift: meatpacking
John D. Rockefeller: oil
Andrew Carnegie: steel

Industrialization Word Search (p. 61)

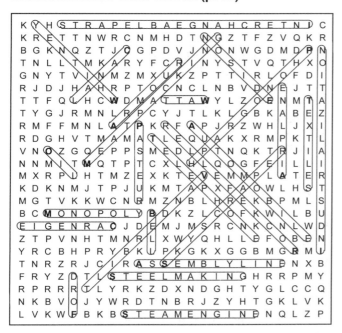

Who Invented It? (p. 62)

1. W.H. Hoover
2. King Camp Gillette
3. Samuel Morse
4. Alessandro Volta
5. Clarence Birdseye
6. Henry Ford
7. Alexander Graham Bell
8. Isaac Singer
9. Rudolf Diesel
10. James Watt
11. Karl Benz

The Roaring Twenties Time Line Activity (p. 64)

1. 1926
2. Calvin Coolidge
3. Nineteenth Amendment, 1920
4. "Steamboat Willie"
5. 1929
6. *Reader's Digest, Time, The New Yorker*
7. three
8. Woodrow Wilson
9. Herbert Hoover
10. 1920
11. Wheaties™
12. 1919
13. The "Grand Ole Opry"
14. neon signs
15. 1922

Prohibition Becomes the Law (p. 66)
Matching
1. b   2. c   3. a

Warren G. Harding (p. 67)
Constructed Response

Charles R. Forbes, a personal friend of Harding's, was tried for bribery and conspiracy. He authorized hundreds of millions of dollars for overpriced materials, sites, and construction.

Secretary of the Interior Albert Fall was convicted of accepting an illegal payment of $400,000 in return for turning over two valuable tracts of land to private oil companies.

Attorney General Harry Daughtery stood trial twice for conspiring to defraud the government by selling government favors.

Women Finally Allowed to Vote (p. 68)
1–2. Answers will vary. See map.
3. With the exception of New York, none of the eastern or southern states had allowed full suffrage before the Nineteenth Amendment was passed. The states that did were all west of the Mississippi River.

Flaming Youth (p. 69)
Constructed Response

The young people were nicknamed the "Flaming Youth" because they lived for pleasure, enjoyed fast-paced music and vigorous dances, wore "scandalous" fashions and hairdos, and developed a taste for zany stunts like flagpole sitting and marathon dances.

Graphic Organizer

Flappers of the Twenties: wore plunging necklines, hemlines above the knees, and makeup; cut their hair short; smoked cigarettes

Teenagers of Today: answers will vary

Americans on the Go (p. 70)
True or False
1. F   2. T   3. T   4. F   5. T   6. F
7. T   8. T   9. T   10. T

Welcome to the Jazz Age (p. 72)
Constructed Response

Dixieland jazz was played mostly by whites. Chicago jazz evolved from the New Orleans style, but there was more of an emphasis on soloists, and it often featured saxophones, pianos, and vocalists. Also it had tenser rhythms and more complicated textures.

Louis Armstrong (p. 73)
Technology in the Classroom
"Hello, Dolly"

John Calvin Coolidge (p. 74)
Research
1. July 4, 1872, in Plymouth Notch, Vermont
2. Silent Cal
3. Republican
4. Lawyer
5. "Keep Cool with Coolidge"

What Could You Buy for a Dollar? (p. 75)

Twenties: Movie ticket - 10 cents
             Gallon of milk - 58 cents
             Pack of gum - 5 cents
             Candy bar - 5 cents
             Ice cream bar - 5 cents
Today's prices will vary.

Learning a New Language: Jive Talk (p. 76)
Matching

1. b	2. m	3. h	4. f	5. l	6. r
7. a	8. g	9. n	10. c	11. o	12. q
13. e	14. p	15. d	16. k	17. i	18. j

Twenties Internet Scavenger Hunt (p. 77)

1. The Green Bay Packers
2. Chicago Bears
3. balloon tires
4. a dog
5. The Harlem Globetrotters
6. Margaret Gorman
7. Nellie Tayloe Ross
8. *The Spirit of St. Louis*
9. 33 hours and 32 minutes
10. Alexander Fleming

Who's Who? (p. 79)
Matching

1. singer (opera)	2. (jazz) musician
3. dancer/actor	4. author
5. actor/film maker	6. pilot
7. boxer	8. film maker
9. pilot	10. composer
11. (jazz) musician	12. football player
13. actress	14. magician
15. golfer	16. boxer
17. anthropologist	18. (jazz) musician
19. Olympic medal winner (track)	
20. baseball player	21. (jazz) singer
22. author	23. tennis player
24. boxer	
25. Olympic medal winner (swimmer)/actor	

The Other Side of the Coin (p. 80)
Graphic Organizer
All would be Then & Now except playing video games, watching television, and riding skateboards, which would be Now only.

Review the Twenties (p. 82)
Matching

1. c	2. h	3. a	4. f	5. g	6. d
7. j	8. i	9. e	10. b		

True or False

1. F	2. T	3. F	4. T	5. T	6. F
7. T	8. F	9. F	10. F		

The Great Depression Time Line Activity (p. 84)

1. 1932 in Lake Placid, New York
2. *LIFE* and *Look*
3. *Snow White and the Seven Dwarfs*
4. Franklin D. Roosevelt
5. 1931
6. half
7. Empire State Building
8. Cost rose from 2 cents to 3 cents
9. Frances Perkins
10. 13 million
11. 40 cents an hour
12. Twenty-first
13. 1935
14. electric typewriters
15. *Funnies on Parade*

The Crash Heard Around the World (p. 86)
Graphic Organizer

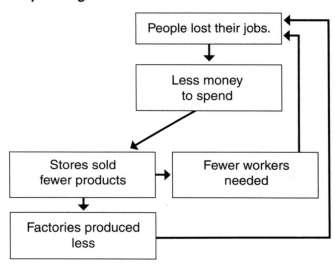

Franklin D. Roosevelt (p. 91)
Matching

1. e	2. d	3. a	4. b	5. c

Fill in the Blanks

1. mother	2. sports	3. Harvard
4. crutches	5. governor	

Constructed Response
Until he was 14, he had private tutors. His mother supervised his education. He married Eleanor even though his mother advised against it. After he had polio, his mother wanted him to retire from politics, but he didn't.

President Roosevelt (p. 93)
Matching
1. b   2. e   3. c   4. a   5. d
Fill in the Blanks
1. 13,000,000   2. New Deal   3. Prohibition
4. 1936   5. fourth
Constructed Response
Roosevelt wanted people to see him as a strong leader. To conceal his disability, he was seated first at dinner parties, and his wheelchair was removed before guests arrived. The press did not report on his condition and published pictures of him standing.

Math Facts (p. 96)
1. $24   2. $1,248
3. Answer will depend on current year.
4. 4,726 miles   5. 7 hours
6. $0.50 per hour   7. $169
8. $15   9. $360
10. 36%   11. 15,856,593
12. 17,064,426

Isolationism (p. 98)
Cause and Effect
1. There was a flood of immigration to the United States from these nations.
2. People decided to ignore the problems of other countries.

New Deal Programs (p. 99)
Graphic Organizer
CCC: established in 1933; provided needy young men with jobs in national parks; unemployed, unmarried men between 17 and 23 were eligible; paid $30 a month; lived in work camps
Both: New Deal program
WPA: began in 1935; employed workers in road maintenance and construction of buildings and facilities; jobs for artists, writers, and actors/actresses

An Alphabet Soup of New Deal Programs (p. 100)
1. Federal Deposit Insurance Corporation
2. Tennessee Valley Authority
3. Federal Emergency Relief Administration
4. Agricultural Adjustment Administration
5. Home Owners' Loan Corporation
6. National Recovery Administration

Desperate Times, Desperate People, Desperate Actions (p. 102)
Matching
1. d   2. e   3. b   4. a   5. c

Fill in the Blanks
1. apples   2. street vendors   3. foreclosures
4. shelters   5. jobs
Constructed Response
In 1930, there was an oversupply of fruit. The Apple Shippers Association sold apples on credit to people who were unemployed. The unemployed would stand on street corners and sell the apples for five cents. This helped the Association sell more apples that would have gone to waste. It helped give the unemployed some income. Consumers could buy fresh apples.

George W. Norris (p. 104)
Matching
1. e   2. a   3. d   4. c   5. b
Fill in the Blanks
1. statesmen   2. senator, Nebraska
3. utilities   4. 30 dams   5. Twentieth
Constructed Response
Nine of the high dams created huge man-made lakes and provided electricity to a poor region. Parks were created, trees and grass were planted over eroded areas, and soil fertility was restored.

Let's Listen to the Radio (p. 105)
Constructed Response
They listened to political speeches, sports programs, weather forecasts, situation comedies, dramas, soap operas, advertisements, and plays.

Eleanor Roosevelt (p. 106)
1. mother, maternal grandmother
2. ten
3. London, England
4. Franklin Roosevelt
5. My Day
6. Lake Placid
7. Lincoln Memorial
8. United Nations
9. Roosevelt
10. former U.S. President Theodore Roosevelt

The Dust Bowl (p. 108)
Cause and Effect
Thousands of families migrated west in search of a better life.

Conditions Get Worse (p. 109)
Map Skills
1. Utah, Arizona, New Mexico, Colorado, Wyoming, Nebraska, Iowa, Missouri, Tennessee, Arkansas, and Louisiana
2. New Mexico, Texas, Oklahoma, and Kansas
3. Wyoming, Nebraska, and Iowa

A Cottage For Sale (p. 110)
Word Search Puzzle

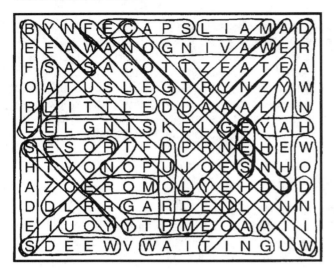

Thirties Internet Scavenger Hunt (p. 112)
1. Kaw
2. Babe Ruth
3. Ronald Reagan
4. tax evasion
5. The "William Tell Overture"
6. Jay Silverheels
7. Gene Autry
8. Band leader
9. Arthur Jacob Arshawasky

Review the Thirties (p. 113)
Matching

1. d   2. g   3. e   4. f   5. h
6. b   7. c   8. a

True or False

1. F   2. T   3. F   4. F   5. T
6. F   7. F   8. T   9. F   10. T